Discovering
FLORIDA'S COAST

From the Emerald Northwest to Miami's Biscayne Jewel and Beyond

DOUG ALDERSON

PINEAPPLE PRESS
Palm Beach, Florida

D1127681

Pineapple Press, Inc.
An imprint of Globe Pequot, the trade division of
The Rowman & Littlefield Publishing Group, Inc.
4501 Forbes Blvd., Ste. 200
Lanham, MD 20706
www.rowman.com

Distributed by NATIONAL BOOK NETWORK

British Library Cataloguing in Publication Information Available

Library of Congress Cataloging-in-Publication Data

Names: Alderson, Doug, author.
Title: Discovering Florida's coast : from the Emerald Northwest to Miami's Biscayne jewel and beyond / Doug Alderson.
Description: Palm Beach : Pineapple Press, Florida, [2023] | Includes bibliographical references and index.
Identifiers: LCCN 2022028062 (print) | LCCN 2022028063 (ebook) | ISBN 9781683343356 (paperback) | ISBN 9781683343363 (epub)
Subjects: LCSH: Florida—Guidebooks. | Coasts—Florida.
Classification: LCC F309.3 .A558 2023 (print) | LCC F309.3 (ebook) | DDC 917.5904—dc23/eng/20220629
LC record available at https://lccn.loc.gov/2022028062
LC ebook record available at https://lccn.loc.gov/2022028063

CONTENTS

Introduction   1

1   The Emerald Northwest   9

2   Forgotten No More   16

3   The Wild Nature Coast   31

4   Mangroves, Culture, and Sun   43

5   Calusa Whispers   57

6   Everglades Wilderness   66

7   The Keys: A Place Like No Other   78

8   Miami's Biscayne Jewel   91

9   Of Shipwrecks and Spanish Treasure   103

10   From Rockets to Kayaks   112

11   St. Augustine's Living History   124

12   Bluffs and Tidal Mazes   135

13   Helping Our Coast   147

Bibliography   150

Index   156

About the Author   164

Florida Shore
By Doug Alderson

I walk the Florida shore
Where Native Americans fished
And conquistadores landed
Where fiddler crabs still scurry into marsh
And raccoons stalk at sunset.
For eons, human and animal footprints have
*   been washed away with each tide*
Twice daily
The shore refreshed and renewed.

Entrance to St. Petersburg Beach lined with native vegetation.

INTRODUCTION

Florida has numerous quaint RV parks along its coast, such as the Ho-Hum RV Park along the Forgotten Coast.

The charm of Florida cannot be put on paper. Once felt, however, it lingers with its victim so long as he draws breath. It is a composite of an infinite variety of physical elements blended with an undefinable something for which there is no word in our language, something almost spiritual in its power to instill that sense of general well-being, the feeling that all's right with the world and with one's soul which the old Greeks called "euphoria."

—FRANK PARKER STOCKBRIDGE AND JOHN HOLLIDAY PERRY, *SO THIS IS FLORIDA*, 1938

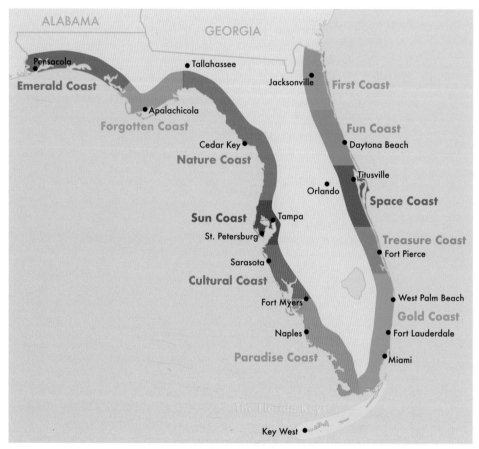

Florida's coast broken down by its regional names. COMPILED FROM VARIOUS SOURCES.

Wanted

Field Director for long-distance paddling trail along Florida's entire coast.

Job Duties: kayaking; taking GPS readings; kayaking; plotting routes on a map; kayaking; determining locations of rest stops, launches, points of interest, potable water, resupply opportunities, campsites, and motels; kayaking; coordinating with local paddlers, paddling clubs, outfitters, government officials, land and water managers, and coworkers; kayaking.

For a water-loving outdoors person, putting together a long-distance paddling trail is a dream job. For three years, my job for the state of Florida was to scout the 1,515-mile Florida Circumnavigational Saltwater Paddling Trail from emerald Gulf waters along the Florida Panhandle, around North America's southernmost tip at Key West, to historic Fort Clinch State Park along the Georgia border on the Atlantic side. My travels encompassed every mile of Florida's coast and every Florida coastal habitat type, from barrier island dune systems to salt marsh to mangroves. Highlights included island hopping along the "Forgotten Coast," paddling the remote Ten Thousand Islands in South Florida, and experiencing the beauty of a place with an unflattering name—Mosquito Lagoon. But I found all parts of Florida's coast to have distinct characteristics and scenic beauty. The more I explored, the more my appreciation deepened, and it continued long after my dream job ended.

But my love affair with Florida's coast began far earlier than the Circumnavigational Trail. Within a few months of moving to Florida in 1968, my parents devised a plan to tour the state with a rented pop-up camper, staying mostly at state parks. We moved down the East Coast all the way to Key West and returned by way of the West Coast. We boated, snorkeled, fished, swam, and hiked, and what a grand adventure it was! For newbies from a Chicago suburb, Florida's coast was a dynamic, ever-changing canvas. We arrived home in Tallahassee with sand in our shoes and salt in our spirits. It has never left.

The Florida Circumnavigational Saltwater Paddling Trail.
OFFICE OF GREENWAYS AND TRAILS, FLORIDA DEPARTMENT OF ENVIRONMENTAL PROTECTION.

Great blue heron at Fort De Soto Park along Tampa Bay in early morning.

Florida's coast conjures up images of emerald-tinted waters of Pensacola and Destin, the high rugged dunes of Cape San Blas, the remote barrier islands of the Forgotten Coast, and the tidal mazes and underwater sea grass prairies along the Nature Coast. Sandy shores and palm trees—along with mangrove jungles—begin around Pinellas County and continue south all the way to Marco Island. And just when you thought these classic beaches that alternate between carefully protected parks and human enclaves will go on forever, there is remoteness and wilderness again in the Ten Thousand Islands and Everglades National Park, where one can travel days without seeing a building higher than a Seminole-style chickee at a primitive campsite.

The unique Florida Keys is a world unto its own with Gulf waters in Florida Bay joining the vast Atlantic Ocean at gaps between islands often marked by historic Roman-style bridges originally built for Henry Flagler's railroad more than a century ago.

Miami's Biscayne Bay includes wild islands like Elliott Key and Boca Chita Key as well as man-made islands planted with native palms and a skyline unsurpassed in the Sunshine State.

Moving up the East Coast, cities are interspersed with wild beaches with tall dunes and some that feature unique rock formations such as at Blowing Rocks Preserve near Jupiter and Washington Oaks Gardens State Park near St. Augustine. Some of the country's most magnificent lighthouses are found along the East Coast, too, ones that you can climb such as at Jupiter Inlet and Anastasia to gain a bird's eye view of a coastal panorama.

The Big Talbot/Amelia Island area is a fitting terminus for Florida's East Coast with its high, live oak-covered bluffs and rich history.

The human culture of Florida's coast is as varied as the terrain, ranging from rustic fishing hamlets that have tapped the sea's bounty for generations to condo communities consisting mostly of people originating from colder climates. Select coastal towns and cities are featured in the book as well. For the purposes of this book, Florida's coast has been divided into 12 distinct segments, generally following names and boundaries applied by local and regional tourist promotion entities, while the final chapter describes ways you can help Florida's coast.

The central theme of the book is how Florida's coast is a unique blending of beauty, natural history, and human culture, showcasing why it is the most dynamic and varied in the nation.

As you explore Florida's coast with me in this book, I also urge you to visit in person and make your adventure unique, and to take it slowly. Don't miss the leaping dolphins, cavorting manatees, or diving pelicans. Catch every sunrise and sunset. And meet the people, especially those salty characters who have made the coast their permanent home. You'll likely need many journeys because one can never take it all in.

The narrow strip of Gulf shore between Panama City and Pensacola is the popular weekend and summer vacation ground for many Alabamans who travel less than 100 miles to achieve a salt-water tan. Along the highways to the shore automobiles loaded with bathing, fishing, and golf paraphernalia are numerous from Friday to Sunday. Cottages, hotels, and rooming houses are filled; Saturday night dances are gala affairs at Panama City and Pensacola hotels, and at the many beach casinos between the cities.

—*FLORIDA: A GUIDE TO THE SOUTHERNMOST STATE,*
FEDERAL WRITERS PROJECT, 1939

A couple walks on St. Andrews Beach near Panama City late in the day.

1

THE EMERALD NORTHWEST

To grasp how much Florida's Emerald Coast has evolved over the past century, look at the example of Norwegian sailor Theodore Tollofsen who shipwrecked during a hurricane on what is now St. Andrews State Park in 1929. Fondly known as "Teddy the Hermit," Tollofsen found the place so remote—there was no bridge to the Grand Lagoon—that he decided to stay permanently. He remained until his death in 1954. His makeshift shack, one that utilized elements of his beached sailboat, formerly stood between park campsites 101 and 102.

Coastal land in the area was inexpensive during those times. When the state of Florida acquired the first 302 acres for St. Andrews State Park from the federal government in 1937, the bargain price was $2.50 an acre. As an archeologist friend pointed out to me, many parts of the Florida coast were considered harsh environments in historic times. They were places to fish, make salt and turpentine, and maybe take a dip, but not to make lengthy stays or live permanently. Coastal environments bore the brunt of storms, some so severe that the very sand foundation of a structure would wash away. As a result, the coastline would constantly shift with passes to bays and estuaries either opening or closing. The phenomenon still occurs today, even more so as hurricanes become stronger and more frequent due to climate change. Most modern coastal buildings, however, are built to higher standards, and federal flood insurance allows for rebuilding. Air conditioning and mosquito control have also played prominent roles in the development of Florida's coast and interior.

Colorful 1930s–era "Rainbow Cabins" at Camp Helen State Park.

Despite the risks, the lure of the Panhandle's sugar sand beaches and clear emerald waters created a building and tourist boom, starting in the 1930s with the "gay-colored summer cottages" that lined the dunes west of Panama City Beach, according to the Federal Writers Project guide to Florida in 1939. You can still see carefully preserved examples of these colorful beach cottages at Camp Helen State Park, once a resort for employees of an Alabama textile mill. Because these Panhandle coastal areas catered heavily to folks from Alabama, especially in summer when south Florida was experiencing its down season, the area was often dubbed "the redneck riviera." Now, visitors from other southeastern states and Canada are as much a part of the summer scene as Alabamans.

A major lure of the Emerald Coast was and is the sand itself, considered some of the whitest in the world, like powdered sugar. It sparkles with quartz particles carried down from the southern Appalachians for millennia by the Chattahoochee and Apalachicola Rivers, starting when the mountains were as tall as any in the world today, making these beaches unique. The sand actually squeaks when you walk on it! Bags of the sand are even sold online for crafts. These quartz sands extend westward from the Apalachicola River to Pensacola Pass.

And what about the emerald waters of the Emerald Coast? The water's clarity is due to geography. The region is far enough away from where the Mississippi River empties into the Gulf so as not to be muddied, and the emerald color is primarily due to the sun reflecting off harmless, microscopic algae. When seen against the white sand, an emerald hue seems to glow!

The name of the Emerald Coast itself was coined by a middle school student in 1983 as part of a contest for a new area slogan. Andrew Dier won $50 for a label that helped usher in untold millions in tourist revenue. And while the label was initially claimed only by Okaloosa and Walton Counties, the Emerald Coast now applies to that stretch of shoreline from Pensacola to Panama City, covering five counties.

Since the first tourist boom of the 1930s, Emerald Coast attractions, gift shops, restaurants, and motels have been reinvented numerous times, the buildings getting taller and more expansive with each incarnation. Protective dunes, quaint coastal roads, mom and pop establishments, funky roadside attractions, and shoreline forests have been the primary sacrifices of such evolution.

Author Tim Hollis tried to capture tourist development patterns of the Emerald Coast in *Florida's Miracle Strip*, concluding: "It is true that trying to document

Evening along the Emerald Coast at Fort Walton Beach.

the development of a tourist capital is made extremely difficult by the tendency of such areas to care only about the here and now. Compounding the problem is that, quite often, there seems to be a certain amount of embarrassment among the locals when it comes to discussing the tackier elements of the region's reputation when, ironically, those are the elements that linger most fondly in visitors' memories, and they do so long after economic reality has made them obsolete."

Panama City Beach had by far the largest number of tourist-oriented attractions, ones that included Western theme parks such as Tombstone Territory and Petticoat Junction, the Miracle Strip Amusement Park, "Snake-a-Torium" reptile center, and several funky miniature golf courses. Like shifting sands on a beach, most are gone now, but the 1950s-era Goofy Golf, where giant colorful dinosaurs and other features are part of the course, is the last of its kind to survive. And dolphins still leap as they have for decades during daily shows at Gulf World Marine Park and at Gulfarium in Fort Walton Beach.

Another transformation along the Emerald Coast involves "new urbanist" master-planned communities such as Seaside and WaterColor. Seaside, adjacent to Grayton Beach State Park, is where parts of the movie *The Truman Show* featuring Jim Carrey was filmed. In the movie, Truman Burbank lives a perfect life in an idyllic small town, the unwitting star of a reality television show until he slowly figures out the scenario and plans an escape.

The main attraction of Seaside is its small-town feel—town squares, walkable neighborhoods, and cracker-style architecture. There are no looming condos here! Most houses are built with wood frames and feature wide roof overhangs, big porches, and windows that actually open for cross ventilation. Of course, there are modern innovations, such as central heat and air, and prices far beyond the reach of a cracker homesteader. Seaside lots that sold for $15,000 in 1981 will now fetch more than $1 million. The principles of New Urbanism that Seaside developed so well have been emulated by hundreds of planned communities in the United States, including nearby WaterColor. WaterColor was built by the St. Joe Company, a former tree farm giant and pulp manufacturer turned developer.

The opening page for WaterColor's website reads like a description of Andy Griffith's Mayberry with a coastal feel: "A gulf breeze welcomes you, offering a sense of relaxation. Neighbors gather on expansive porches over lemonade. There's an exceptional feeling of comfort and familiarity in the WaterColor community. It cultivates a true sense of place that is timeless, authentic, and welcoming for generations to come." Unlike Mayberry, residents can access a boathouse with paddleboards, kayaks, and fishing equipment; an outdoor amphitheater; a lakeside pool; a bike barn; and more. But could Aunt Bee, Andy, Barney, and Gomer afford to live in WaterColor or in most communities along today's Emerald Coast? In a pattern playing out throughout Florida, most workers in coastal communities have to commute from inland areas where housing is less expensive.

One inexpensive way to see the Emerald Coast is by kayak, camping along the way. Big Lagoon State Park near Pensacola marks the beginning of the 1,515-mile

Florida Circumnavigational Saltwater Paddling Trail, a mapped route that reaches around Florida's entire coastline. You can kayak camp almost every night. Thousands paddle short stretches of the trail every year, but only a few hardy souls tackle the entire trail. It's not an easy journey, involving a bit more than sitting on a front porch in WaterColor sipping lemonade with neighbors. Bugs, storms, high winds, and waves can all be encountered. Then there are the sore muscles, the sunburn, and the salt and sand that seem to get into everything.

"This trip is an incredible challenge," said Mary Mangiapia, who took just over three months to complete the trail in 2014. "Along the way, I have encountered 10-foot seas and numerous storms. I even cracked a Kevlar bulkhead while crossing Tampa Bay in big waves, and I also have teeth marks in my kayak from a bull shark."

So, why do it? The reasons given by those who have completed the trail, a group known as "thru-paddlers," are many.

Besides her trip's challenges, Mary Mangiapia becomes philosophic. "Completing the trip and doing a large part of it solo helped me feel more confident in myself and my abilities. I found great peace being in nature and in living by the rhythms of the winds and tides. That has carried on well beyond the trip.

"I saw lots of wildlife, and I treasure the memory of dolphins escorting me through a storm. I met kind people from all walks of life who helped me along the

Matt Keene signs trail logbook at Big Lagoon State Park in January 2009 as the first person to complete the entire Florida Circumnavigational Saltwater Paddling Trail.

The historic Wesley House in Eden Gardens State Park overlooks Choctawhatchee Bay.

way and I am still friends with many of them. Even though I am a Florida native and have lived here my whole life, the trip allowed me to see areas of the state that I would have never seen otherwise."

Matt Keene landed at Big Lagoon State Park in early 2009 after almost four months of paddling, becoming the first person to complete the entire trail. He did the trail in reverse, starting at Fort Clinch State Park at the top of Florida's northeast coast along the Georgia border. "As you progress in your journey, your needs become simplified, and with that comes a simpler view of living your life," he said. "You shed the weight of civilization—the stress, the doubt, the body fat. . . . Your confidence rises, and you learn to live day by day."

Jodi Eller, who completed the trail in segments over several years, added, "The trail is amazing. It goes through so many different ecosystems. How the beaches change along the trail is just incredible. The trail made me a stronger paddler and it also redefined who I am in a way, bringing me back to the essence of being human. It's a powerful experience to go through."

Along the Emerald Coast, the Circumnavigational Trail skirts inside protective barrier islands from Pensacola to Destin. Then, one has a choice: paddle in open water along the beaches to Mexico Beach and Cape San Blas, or take the Intracoastal Waterway from Choctawhatchee Bay all the way to Apalachicola. Most opt for the Intracoastal unless they are highly skilled at open water paddling, or very fortunate with the weather. The Intracoastal involves skipping much of the emerald waters of the Emerald Coast for a more interior route.

The majority of people who enjoy the waters off the Emerald Coast are recreational anglers with high-powered boats. Destin is billed as "the world's luckiest fishing village," a phrase coined by Florida governor Leroy Collins in 1956 when he caught a 19-pound king mackerel on only a 15-minute photo-op boat trip around East Pass. When asked about his incredible luck by a reporter, Collins smiled and replied, "Not if you're fishing out of Destin. Them boys live with the fish. Destin's the world's luckiest fishing village."

So, whether one is fortunate enough to live full time or part time along the Emerald Coast, or to simply fish, kayak, or lie on the beach for a few hours or days, the lure of quartz sands and emerald waters will surely continue to grow as it has for decades.

Unspoiled coastal forest along the Emerald Coast in Topsail Hill Preserve State Park.

2
FORGOTTEN NO MORE

Dawn paddler along Piney Island near Panacea on the Forgotten Coast.

One generally thinks of lighthouses as being erected at strategic locations and standing strong for centuries due to their solid construction. But that hasn't been the case with the Cape St. George Light along the Forgotten Coast. First erected in 1833 near West Pass between Apalachicola Bay and the Gulf, it was moved in 1848 because approaching boats from the east found it difficult to see. Three years later, the lighthouse was felled by a powerful hurricane, so a third lighthouse was built more than 400 yards from the Gulf. Here it remained through Civil War and hurricanes until coastal erosion gradually stripped away the beach, allowing waves to relentlessly pound the lighthouse base. Eventually, the structure tilted and then toppled in 2005. The lighthouse lay in pieces in the surf, but with community support and public and private funding, the salvageable remnants were relocated to nearby St. George Island in a public park where the lighthouse was painstakingly reconstructed according to the original 1852 plans.

"We tried to look at the bright side of it, and said 'Well, if you can dig a dinosaur up out of the ground and put the bones back together in a museum, we can dig this lighthouse up and put the pieces back together,'" Dennis Barnell, president of the St. George Lighthouse Association, told *USA Today*. "It's somewhat of a miracle."

A replica of the original lighthouse keeper's house was also built and serves as a museum and gift shop. Throngs of people visit in good weather and pay a few bucks to climb the 92 stairs for a panoramic view of the coast and bay.

Following the coast on our left, numerous reefs of large and very fat oysters continually obstructed our progress. We gathered a bushel with our hands in a very few minutes; but as the wind commenced to blow most spitefully, and the heavy forests of palms on the low shore offered a pleasant shelter, we disembarked about sunset in a magnificent grove of palmetto-trees, spending a pleasant evening in feasting upon the delicious bivalves, roasted and upon the half shell.

—NATHANIEL H. BISHOP, DESCRIBING A ROWBOAT TRIP ACROSS
APALACHICOLA BAY AS PART OF A 2,600-MILE JOURNEY
CHRONICLED IN *FOUR MONTHS IN A SNEAK-BOX,* 1879

The reconstructed Cape St. George Lighthouse on St. George Island.

A few years ago, while kayak camping on the remote and unpopulated Cape St. George, I met two people with family history related to the lighthouse, Joe Barber and Eleanor Hillman, brother and sister. They had taken a boat to the island from Carrabelle. Their grandfather, Edward G. Porter, was keeper of the Cape St. George Light from the late 1800s until his untimely death in 1913. He owned the island at the time. They said the island once had a schoolhouse and several cottages before being taken over by the military in the 1940s so soldiers could practice beach assaults before being deployed to Europe or South Pacific islands.

The spiraling wood staircase of the Cape St. George Lighthouse.

While the state of Florida paid $8.5 million for the 9-mile-long Cape St. George in 1977, Joe remembered when "you couldn't give away these islands because of taxes."

Joe worked as a commercial fisherman and guide for most of his life. "We'd go out for three or four days at a time," he said. "We hardly ever came back with under 1,500 pounds of fish with three men working. One time, three of us in a little 36-foot boat caught 4,270 pounds of snapper in less than 24 hours." They returned to the site and caught another 3,900 pounds of mixed grouper and snapper. "I've made a living on eight different boats," he concluded. He also captained the St. George Island Ferry for several years before a bridge to the island was constructed.

Later, I learned how Joe aided in the rescue of 14 survivors of the English tanker HMS *Empire Mica* that had been torpedoed by a German U-boat in 1942 about 20 miles off Cape San Blas. He and a friend towed in another rescue boat that had run out of gas in Apalachicola Bay. "Actually, I helped pull the survivors in," he said in *Voices of the Apalachicola* by Faith Eidse. "Some of them were hurt, some of 'em just had their underclothes on, they had to abandon the ship so quick. Some of 'em had jumped down in their lifeboats and hurt their legs and ankles." Thirty-three sailors died in the attack. The *Empire Mica* has since become a reef that attracts numerous fish and other sea life and is considered a living memorial.

Joe ended his career on the water as a boat captain for the Florida State University Marine Laboratory at St. Theresa a few miles from Carrabelle. He passed away in 2014 at age 92, but his contribution to the rich fabric of the Forgotten Coast lives on.

Original Fresnel lens of the Crooked River Lighthouse, manufactured in Paris in 1894, resembles an alien face.

The Forgotten Coast has a wealth of history, and one seems to run into it at every turn, whether it is meeting one of the coast's old-timers, climbing the reconstructed Cape St. George Light or the original Crooked River Lighthouse near

Carrabelle, touching old-growth coastal slash pines on St. George Island that were once "cat faced" to collect sap for turpentining, or witnessing the many eroding Indian middens on St. Vincent Island that are spilling out into Apalachicola Bay. And along Highway 98 near Lanark Village, it is easy to envision US soldiers training for amphibious assaults during World War II. Camp Gordon Johnston, located along the mainland side of Apalachicola Bay from 1942 to 1946, trained 250,000 men in amphibious operations. Due to bugs and heat, the camp had a nickname for their location that no chamber of commerce representative would dare whisper— "Hell by the Sea."

"It was a tough place to be, but in retrospect, it was good because it really conditioned us for the battles we fought in New Guinea, the Netherlands and the East Indies," recalled former camp resident Henry C. Allan in *Tallahassee Magazine*. You can learn all about it at the Camp Gordon Johnston Museum in Carrabelle.

The trademarked name of this coast—Forgotten Coast—is relatively new, coined in the early 1990s by the Apalachicola Bay Chamber of Commerce to attract tourists seeking a quiet retreat. The name proved successful. Visitors are increasingly finding this stretch of shore to their liking. Unspoiled coastal peninsulas, wild barrier islands, dynamic bays and estuaries, and unmarred vistas of salt marsh, tree islands, and winding tidal creeks stretch from Mexico Beach to St. Marks, and all invite exploration.

The tall dunes of Cape San Blas in St. Joseph Peninsula State Park make for a fitting bookend on the western end of the Forgotten Coast. The cape is a long, thin tail of land, curling around St. Joe Bay and tapering into the Gulf. It is perhaps the wildest peninsula left in Florida, extending over 8 miles. The dunes on

Deer along remote dunes of St. Joseph Peninsula State Park.

the Gulf side are up to three stories tall. When standing on top of one of those high dunes, the peninsula appears to be a still sea of green, gray, and white. The interior is made up of tough bonsai-like pines, twisted shrubs, and fragrant wild rosemary. The plants stubbornly try to survive against torturing winds, salt, and storms, and some don't make it, especially near the dunes. Over time, the dunes will move and roll like slow moving waves, robbing roots of essential soil, seeming to freeze their dying gasps in midair.

Hurricane Michael walloped this section of coast and nearby Mexico Beach in 2018, and the region is slowly recovering. Michael was only a tropical storm when it moved into the Gulf of Mexico's unseasonably high 84-degree waters on October 7, 2018. But then Michael began to gain strength—Category 1, then a 2. By the morning of October 11, Michael was a Category 5 hurricane and bearing down with 160-mile-an-hour winds and a 20-foot storm surge. An announcer on the Weather Channel promised a "swamp of destruction." The storm's barometric pressure was approaching that of Hurricane Andrew in 1992.

Mexico Beach, Panama City, and even inland communities such as Marianna experienced catastrophic devastation. "Everything is just gone!" exclaimed a woman in Mexico Beach.

Charles Smith, owner of the Gulf View Motel in Mexico Beach, decided to ride out the storm in his motel rather than evacuate. "Then the walls started collapsing in, I was able to get one door open," he said in *Here and Now*. "I grabbed one of my cats, just threw it in the office. It went up to the top stairs, I went back down for the other ones, the door slammed on me. The water went up . . . from 2 feet to 4, to floating me up to the roof. Then I got sucked into the laundry room with the four cats. And then the refrigerator hit me, because everything is floating—you take everything that floats and put it right about four feet where you're at, and it's not standing still. It is moving.

Diving pelicans at sunset along Cape San Blas.

"I got hit by beds, stoves—because I'm a motel, and I've got kitchenettes, and my neighbor's house was floating into my house. I grabbed that cat I had, I threw it in, then it [water] came in and sucked me back out. I was able to get back into room No. 2. Then the outside wall caved in, once I got up on the refrigerator, 'cause it sucked in and jammed into the bathroom. I was able to get back up onto the refrigerator. I went to reach for my cat, the wall broke through and the cats just were on the bed, and they just floated out."

Smith vowed to rebuild. The town's other motels were destroyed, too.

Nick Hooppell, a Marianna man, described the hurricane as a bomb going off. Three trees fell on his house in a 10-minute span. "We were breaking down," he said in a *Tallahassee Democrat* article. "We were crying. I mean no one was prepared for this. We stood in the room. We prayed. Every time you wanted it to stop it would hit harder and harder and harder."

Hurricane Michael was the worst storm to hit the Florida Panhandle in recorded history, and it closely followed the highly destructive Florence that hit the North Carolina coast the previous month. It goes to reason that if the oceans are still warm by the second hottest September on record, a tropical storm could turn into a hurricane overnight, and ramp up to be a killer.

But the Forgotten Coast (and all of Florida's coast for that matter) has seen many hurricanes over time. People rebuild or move inland. Barrier islands shift and slowly regenerate dunes, trees, sea oats, and other vegetation. Birds and animals rebound. Peaceful scenes return, the destruction nearly forgotten. The coast is dynamic.

The largest island along the Forgotten Coast is the triangular-shaped St. Vincent, completely undeveloped and protected as part of a 12,492-acre national wildlife refuge. Native American names for this large land mass are not known. The current name was given by Franciscan friars in 1633 while visiting Apalachee Indians in the area. After the Apalachee Indians were dispersed, killed, or captured by the English and their Creek allies in 1704, Creek and Seminole Indians hunted and occasionally occupied the island throughout the latter half of the 1700s and early 1800s. They lost the island in 1811 as part of the Forbes Grant, a land-for-debt exchange in which the Indians forcibly gave up millions of acres of North Florida. Unlimited credit was alive even then until Indian hunters fell hopelessly behind despite traveling weeks at a time away from their families in search of deer skins, their primary trade commodity.

One of the earliest American owners of the island was George Hatch, who purchased the island at auction for $3,000 and used it for a private hunting and fishing preserve. His 1875 headstone near West Pass is the only marked grave on the island.

Perhaps the most colorful owner was Dr. Ray Pierce, a patent medicine king and developer of the Pierce-Arrow car, who bought the island in 1908. Pierce and his family used the island as a winter resort whereupon they feasted on venison, ducks, fish, oysters, and sea turtle eggs most any day. "I counted 127 deer on one mile stretch of beach," read the journal of Charles Marks, whose father was a caretaker of the island for Dr. Pierce, as recounted in Betty Watts' *The Watery Wilderness of Apalach, Florida*. "On the Gulf beach, it was easy on moonlight nights in the summer to find ten or fifteen turtle crawls in an evening, each containing 150 to

Facing page: Windswept palm forests along the Forgotten and Nature Coasts are slowly being lost due to rising seas.

"Sponge man" greets visitors along the sidewalk of downtown Apalachicola.

300 eggs. Mostly 'yellows,' the eggs were best served scrambled, and were excellent in cakes." Marks said the turtles were large enough for a man to ride on their backs.

Pierce, not satisfied with the abundant native wildlife on the island, began to import nonnative species—zebras, elands, German boars, Japanese deer, ring-necked pheasants, and sambar deer from Asia. Most of the exotics eventually died out or were removed, unable to adapt. Only the elk-sized sambar deer remain.

The Nature Conservancy purchased the island in 1968 for $2.2 million and later sold it to the United States Fish and Wildlife Service for establishment as a wildlife refuge. Primitive-weapons hunts of native deer, hogs, and sambar deer occur in fall and winter. The endangered red wolf was reintroduced in 1990 whereupon wolf families freely roam the uninhabited island, the only wild wolf population in Florida. "The few wolves on St. Vincent Island aren't truly wild, but their instincts are, and I sense that in their voices," wrote Susan Cerulean in her St. Vincent Island memoir *Coming to Pass.* "The female's howl is not directed at me, but if I happen to be in her matrix, the soundscape we share, the wolf's voice rouses me. Our culture has taught us to be afraid of wild animals, and to subdue the natural world. In so doing, we also tamp down our own instinctual selves. We must open to the experience of living in the community of nature—being a part of it, not separate from it, certainly not above it."

St. Vincent, St. George, and Dog Islands mark the end of a chain of barrier islands that were formed by sediments deposited by the Apalachicola and Ochlock-onee Rivers. The numerous wild islands east of Ochlockonee Bay are chunks of land that have been isolated by a millennia of rising sea levels, thus the reason why their shapes are not as elongated. St. George Island State Park and Bald Point State Park are natural highlights.

It is along the Forgotten Coast and Nature Coast where sea level rise is most apparent, partly because there are few sea walls or other man-made structures to mask it. Palms, cedars, slash pine, and other trees are toppling over or they are standing skeletal and bleached, like erect corpses. There is very little sign of young trees growing along the coastal fringes, so marsh will likely take over many coastal forests or, increasingly, mangroves will move in from the south, gaining footholds where they never before existed. Shockingly, the change is happening in just a generation or two and it's not difficult to project how these shorelines might appear in 50 or 100 years.

The barrier islands of the Forgotten Coast form a border around the massive Apalachicola Bay, the recipient of waters from the Apalachicola River, Florida's largest in terms of water volume. I once joined a group of high school students in putting out various seine and plankton nets into the bay and was amazed to discover that every ounce of water teemed with life. We found numerous species of fish and thousands of tiny shrimp and zooplankton. This place where fresh and salt water mixed together felt like a living organism, thus one reason it is a massive spawning area for shrimp and many types of fish that are enjoyed in seafood restaurants throughout Florida.

Studies have shown that the bay supports fisheries in the eastern Gulf of Mexico as far south as Tampa and over 250 miles offshore, contributing billions to the economy. The bay's famed oyster industry collapsed in 2012, however, due to extended drought and increased water use by Southwest Georgia farmers and the city of Atlanta along the upper Apalachicola, Chattahoochee, and Flint River system that feeds the Apalachicola River and bay with vital fresh water. In 2020, in an unprecedented move, wild oyster harvesting was suspended by the state for up to five years while a $20 million oyster reef recovery effort was undertaken. The bay once produced 90 percent of Florida's oysters and 10 percent of the country's, supporting hundreds of oyster harvesters who employed generations-old hand-tonging methods. "Many people don't realize how special Apalachicola is, and how vulnerable the bay is. Historically, it was among the most productive for seafood in North America," said Apalachicola seafood wholesaler Steve Rash. "There may have been a few angry about the ban, but most have accepted there are very few oysters out there anymore." Even before the oyster harvesting ban, Rash was refusing to buy Apalachicola oysters from harvesters, calling them endangered species.

If the bay fully recovers, oyster harvesting will return, but a nagging question remains: what happens during the next drought cycle? A 2021 United States Supreme Court decision in Florida versus Georgia over water use in the river system sided with Georgia. Florida couldn't meet the legal burden of proof to show Georgia was at fault for the bay's collapse, so Georgia water users are not under any legal mandate to employ water conservation measures, even under dire circumstances.

Despite the oyster decline, the seafood capital of the Forgotten Coast is still the town of Apalachicola. It has also emerged as the cultural anchor. Once a bustling port city where steamships brought in cotton, lumber, turpentine, and other products from upriver communities, the town is now a center for both seafood harvesting and distribution and businesses that cater primarily to tourists and seasonal residents. Besides shopping and eating fresh seafood, one can stroll through downtown Apalachicola where many pre–Civil War homes and buildings still stand, including the red brick structure where the Apalachicola Sponge Exchange once thrived in the late 1800s and early 1900s. One visitor commented that several buildings could easily grace the cover of a Faulkner novel. And with the town's stately live oaks and grand vistas of water and marsh, Apalachicola's culture is also intertwined with natural beauty, much like the rest of the Forgotten Coast.

Facing page: Early morning rainbow along Alligator Harbor on the Forgotten Coast.

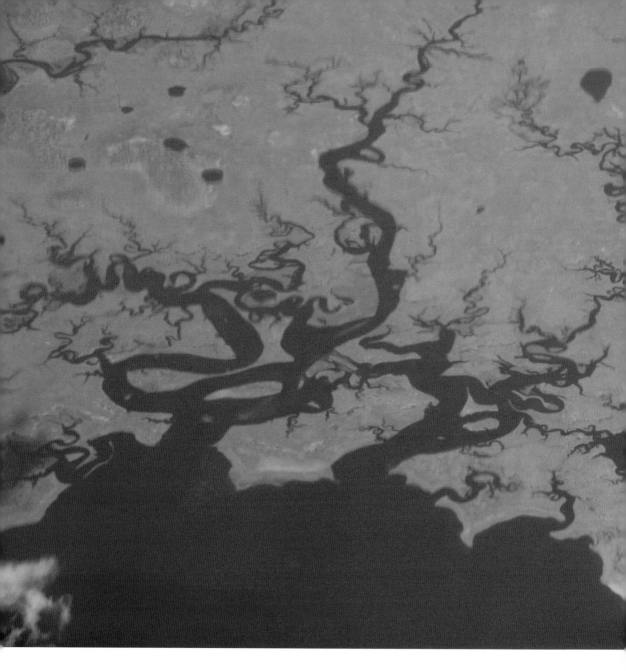

As soon as the school bus dropped us off on Friday, my brothers and I would be off in the woods along the coast. We'd catch fish, gig frogs, cut us some swamp cabbage, and cook everything we caught or gathered in a big coffee can. Our coffee was just some boiled acorn hulls. If it growed and it wasn't poison, we ate it or we tried it. At night, we'd rake up the leaves and cover ourselves up. On Sunday, our parents would gather us up. They'd make us ride in the back of their truck 'cause we stunk so bad.

—LONG-TIME NATURE COAST RESIDENT BILLY SULLIVAN, AKA SHITTY BILL

Aerial view of
unspoiled Nature
Coast tidal creeks.

3

THE WILD NATURE COAST

A vast wet prairie of cordgrass and needlerush stretches for miles along a sinewy shoreline, broken only by occasional tree islands of palm and live oak. An osprey whistles, mullet leap, and a Kemp's ridley sea turtle pokes its head up before quickly submerging. This is the Nature Coast; wild and remote, it is the coastal version of the River of Grass; and, indeed, only the Everglades can claim a wilder reputation in Florida. In a state of more than 21 million people, one can feel incredibly alone here, and yet part of something much larger.

Only a few anglers, crabbers, and sea kayakers explore the many reaches of the Nature Coast. Broadly covering Florida's Big Bend from St. Marks to Pinellas County, this coast covers almost 200 miles and is the transition zone where northern plants and animals give way to the subtropical Caribbean species of peninsular Florida. On a map, it is shown as a 90-degree geographic bend from an east/west linear direction to north/south, but it is much more. Lacking the white sand beaches that have led to dramatic growth in other coastal areas, the Nature Coast's seagrass beds are some of the most expansive and productive in the world. Mazes of tidal creeks wind past marsh and tree islands in scenes reminiscent of what Native Americans and early Spanish explorers witnessed centuries ago.

In parts of the Nature Coast, ages-long biological cycles continue unimpeded. Fiddler crabs are so thick along some marshy shores they appear to be a moving mass of colorful pebbles a thousand deep. Endangered Kemp's ridley sea turtles frequent the shallow waters.

Gulf sturgeon thrill onlookers with dramatic leaps as they enter the Suwannee River for springtime spawning. Exhausted palm warblers on long migratory journeys will often land to rest on boats offshore. And on full or new moon nights in spring, multitudes of horseshoe crabs crawl onto sandy beaches as part of a "nesting aggregation," their brown dome-shaped carapaces collectively resembling a quivering road of helmet-sized cobblestones.

Offshore, beyond the vast shallow seagrass beds, underwater environments can be filled with multicolored sponges, some a fiery orange, along with deep-red sea fans, huge boulders of brain coral, rocks covered with white and purple algae and bryozoans, brown-purple octopuses, pink spiny sea urchins, and yellow starfish. One sponge harvester described it as "like a Lewis Carroll environment," while Panacea author Jack Rudloe, in his book *The Living Dock*, wrote: "No treasure chests brimming with rubies and sapphires, diamonds and emeralds, or gold and silver could compare with it. . . . I felt that I was looking at Pharaoh's treasures."

Fortunately, much of the Nature Coast and its biological riches are in public ownership. Vast tracts include national wildlife refuges, state parks, and state wildlife management areas. Most of the towns interspersed along the Nature Coast—Keaton Beach, Spring Warrior, Horseshoe Beach, Suwannee, Cedar Key, Yankeetown, and Aripeka—are small with an Old Florida flavor, catering to anglers, commercial fishermen, and nature tourists. The largest town is the manatee haven of Crystal River. Many of the rivers emptying into the coast are fed by vast swamps and first-magnitude springs.

In 2003, I had a perfect opportunity to explore part of the Nature Coast firsthand. I worked a stint with the Florida Fish and Wildlife Conservation Commission and helped Liz Sparks, a friend and coworker, finish mapping the Big Bend Saltwater Paddling Trail. For nine days, we paddled 100 miles from the Aucilla River to the town of Suwannee in early September, battling heat and bugs and learning firsthand about the need to have an adequate supply of fresh water between resupply stops. We ran out at one point and started becoming dehydrated.

Despite the hardships, the remote beauty of the Nature Coast astounded us, and the salty characters we met were unforgettable. One was a guy named Billy Sullivan, better known as Shitty Bill. Billy was born and raised near a little hamlet called Spring Warrior. He built a small house on stilts and topped it with a tall crow's nest in sight of the place where he was born. "See that peninsula," he said, "At the very end, where the trees make the shape of a B-29—see, you can make out the tail wing, that's where I was born and raised. That's Jug Island." How many people can say that?

People like Billy were one reason I wrote my first book, *Waters Less Traveled*, published in 2005. He, like many others we met, had deep roots in the region and refused to sell to developers. "What is it to have a lot of money?" Billy said. "You'd never find another place like this." Another nearby resident echoed those same feelings: "I've been all over, but I wouldn't take nothing for this place."

Kayaking along the Nature Coast.

During our explorations, we heard stories of people who once led a nomad-type existence along the Nature Coast. One old-timer called them "the island people" because they often stayed on coastal tree islands in the region. They mostly fished and traded for what they needed, leading a simple life. Some said they had Muscogee Creek/Seminole Indian heritage. A few years ago, at one coastal kayak campsite, a palm-thatched, Indian-style shelter was found, possibly a sign that some island people remained, at least part time.

Many places along the Nature Coast evoke a prehistoric feeling, where one can easily envision a time when sea levels were much lower. The vast sea grass beds were open prairies then, and Paleo Indians used spear-throwing devices known as *atlatls* to hunt mastodons, Columbian mammoths, giant sloths, huge armadillos and tortoises, bears, wolves, wild camels, horses, and a host of other animals. Archeologists have followed former river channels several miles into the Gulf and have found the now underwater sites of Paleo Indian camps.

Archeologist Dan Penton studied several archeological sites along the Nature Coast, mostly ones that were established after many of the large creatures of Paleo times became extinct. "The reason for the coastal encampments was to take advantage of the stable food resources, especially on a seasonal basis," he said. "Jack crevalle, mackerel, and a few other fish were seasonally specific. You could anticipate when they were going to be coming through. They [Native Americans] were working around two parameters. For one, the insect problem was severe at certain times. The other is that it's a pretty raw place to be in the winter."

According to Penton, native people would trek to the coast from as far away as south-central Georgia in late summer or fall to catch fish and harvest scallops and oysters to augment their protein source. Indian shell middens and mounds, some massive such as the 5-acre Shell Mound near Cedar Key, were the result of untold generations of Native Americans feasting on coastal shellfish.

When the first Europeans marched through the region in the 1500s on mis-guided missions to find gold, the millennial coastal lifestyle for Native Americans was disrupted. Disease more than warfare caused an initial massive blow to native populations. Still, native people fought back any way they could, as evidenced by the reception received by Panfilo de Narvaez and his 300 men when they claimed the region for Spain in 1528. Trapped by Apalachee Indians along the "Bay of Horses," what is now likely Apalachee Bay in the St. Marks National Wildlife Refuge, the Spaniards waited for ships that never came. Desperate, killing a horse every third day for food, Cabeza de Vaca, a member of the expedition, wrote in his journal: "We felt certain we would all be stricken, with death the one foresee-able way out; and in such a place, death seemed all the more terrible. Considering our experiences, our prospects, and various plans, we finally concluded to under-take the formidable project of constructing vessels to float away in. This appeared impossible, since none of us knew how to build ships, and we had no tools, iron, forge, oakum, pitch, or rigging, or any of the indispensable items, or anybody to instruct us. Worse still, we had no food to sustain workers."

The Spaniards eventually sailed for Mexico in five makeshift vessels made from native timber, clothing, horse skin, palmetto fiber, and horsehair. Eight years and 6,000 miles later, only four survivors straggled into Mexico City to tell the har-rowing tale.

Hernando De Soto and other conquistadores followed, and many of the sur-viving native people were eventually pacified by Spanish missionaries. For the Apalachee Indians, an English-led raid in 1704 scattered the population with the largest group eventually making their way to Louisiana. Decades later, enticed by good hunting and a lack of European pressure, many Muscogee Creek Indian bands moved into Florida from neighboring states in the mid-1700s, often merg-ing with remnant populations of the original Florida tribes. These native people became known as Seminoles, and they soon began to attract large numbers of escaped slaves and free black people. The Underground Railroad traveled south as much as to northern states and Canada.

A strategic spot for centuries was a Spanish-built fort at the confluence of the Wakulla and St. Marks Rivers where shoreline trees meet the vast marsh and tree islands of the Gulf Coast. First built in 1679, the fort's logs were coated with lime to create the appearance of stone to discourage raiding pirates. This ruse proved unsuccessful, and after several raids, the fort was set afire. Eventually, the Spanish rebuilt the fort out of limestone, but it was still the site of several skirmishes with pirates, British raiders, and, in 1800, British deserter William Augustus Bowles and 400 Seminole and Creek Indian warriors. They held the fort for five weeks before Spanish forces reclaimed it.

An osprey lands with a freshly caught fish along the Nature Coast.

Andrew Jackson and a huge force of American militia and Creek allies were next in the long line of raiders. They captured the fort without a shot in 1818 as part of a sweeping effort to punish Seminole Indians and recapture escaped slaves. Historians would eventually refer to it as the First Seminole War. Jackson's forces had a running battle near the Econfina River with Chief Peter McQueen's band of Creek/Seminole Indians before going on to burn Indian and black, maroon villages along the Suwannee River. Jackson's illegal invasion of Spanish Florida made Spain realize the difficulty in maintaining control of the Sunshine State. They sold it to a growing United States three years later, and Florida became the 27th state in 1845. So, the Nature Coast played a key role in the country's expansion.

No matter what government claimed ownership of Florida, pirates and smugglers found the many remote rivers, islands, and tidal creeks along the Nature Coast to their liking. Stories abound of heavy-laden pirate ships low in the water moving up a Nature Coast river and sailing out again high atop the water. Searches for pirate treasure persist today. Smuggling operations followed, especially during Prohibition when Al Capone's influence was believed to have reached all the way to the Nature Coast. Bootleg liquor was brought up rivers such as the Suwannee and loaded onto train cars and shipped to Chicago and other major cities.

Drug running was a common occurrence in the 1970s with one remote coastal road in Dixie County paved with public funds just so drug planes could have a safe midnight landing strip. Many impoverished local people prospered for a time. "You gotta' understand," one Dixie County resident explained, "You come to a man making a few hundred dollars a month and with a family and offer him several thousand dollars for a night's work; that was tempting."

Sink Creek is one of many unspoiled waterways along the "Road to Nowhere."

The Road to Nowhere, as the former dual-purpose highway is called because it abruptly ends in a salt marsh, is a great birdwatching location. Birds that can be spotted—depending on the season—include white pelicans, black-bellied and piping plovers, willets, marbled godwits, dunlins, dowitchers, vermillion flycatchers, bald eagles, black rails, swallow-tailed kites, and great flocks of wintering or migrating sparrows, warblers, and ducks—186 observed species at last count. And the many creeks the road crosses offer kayaking and boating opportunities and access to an unspoiled coastline and its unparalleled fishing.

One odd historical footnote surrounding the Nature Coast near Apalachee Bay is the "Wakulla Volcano." For decades, mariners and even folks in Florida's capital city of Tallahassee could spot a consistent smoke column emerging from an inland swamp. It became a daytime navigation marker for ships, and its origin sparked creative theories and several fruitless expeditions. Many Florida travel authors in the 19th century mentioned it, such as George M. Barbour in 1882 writing in *Florida for Tourists, Invalids, and Settlers*: "It is in this impenetrable jungle that the famous 'Florida volcano' is supposed to exist, for a column of light, hazy smoke or vapor may be (and has been for years) seen rising from some portion of it, and provokes the conundrum, 'What is it?'" The 1886 Charleston earthquake, one felt throughout the East Coast, put an end to the mysterious smoke plume.

Another historical oddity is the "sidewalk to nowhere" in a tidal zone of remote Bonita Beach. A previous owner in the 1920s built the sidewalk, platted the area for lots, and took photos during low tide. In a classic Florida land swindle, northerners bought the lots sight unseen. When all the lots were sold, the owner skipped town, leaving the crumbling sidewalk to sunning lizards and scurrying fiddler crabs.

Surrounding the sidewalk are small mounds of brick and limestone rubble, usually marked by a cedar tree or two. These were saltworks where iron kettles atop stone ovens boiled down sea water to create salt to cure meat for the Confederate army during the Civil War. The Union army had blockaded salt shipments from abroad, so the demand for salt was great and prices rose dramatically. But making salt was risky business. Union gunboats often shelled the saltworks, or smaller boats came ashore so Union soldiers could destroy them. Besides saltworks, the remote Nature Coast became a hideout for many Confederate deserters and Union sympathizers during the Civil War, and at one point, many of their homes were burned and their families rounded up and placed in a stockade in Tallahassee.

One historical mainstay that still delights visitors is the island town of Cedar Key, a bustling port city built in the mid-to-late 1800s. Sailing vessels and

Seahorse Key near Cedar Key boasts the tallest bluff along the Gulf Coast.

steamships would often fill the harbor, and a railroad built by David Yulee connected Cedar Key to Fernandina on the East Coast. Steam locomotives carrying supplies and passengers chugged across bridges to the four keys that made up the town. Sailors and visitors alike thronged to the town's wharf where saloons, bordellos, gambling establishments, and dance halls were great places to empty a money purse. Skirmishes were commonplace, and like frontier towns of the West, most men carried two pistols and a Bowie knife. One travel writer tagged Cedar Key "the toughest town in the South" while town promoters preferred to call it "the Venice of Florida."

Economically, Cedar Key was riding high, but three things happened. Tampa, with its larger harbor and deeper channel, outcompeted Cedar Key for shipping. Then, the factories that made cedar slats to ship to northern pencil factories began to run out of coastal cedar trees. And if this wasn't enough, a killer hurricane struck in 1896, causing massive damage. Cedar Key quietly withdrew until tourists discovered the town again in the latter half of the 20th century. But these weren't your typical tourists who frequented roadside attractions and, later, Disney World and theme parks. These were nature tourists looking to birdwatch, kayak out to unspoiled islands nearby, take walking tours through the historic district, visit art galleries and art shows, and frequent shops and restaurants that felt like Old Florida. To this day, there isn't a chain restaurant or motel in Cedar Key, and that suits most residents and visitors just fine. Town promoters adopted a slogan, "a place where time stands still."

A contemporary photo of the historic wharf of Cedar Key.

Gulf Coast fritillary butterfly on goldenrod along the Nature Coast.

Manatees congregate at the entrance to Three Sisters Springs in Crystal River.

Farther south, nature lovers flock to Crystal River and Homosassa Springs to see manatees and other wildlife. Manatees congregate in the region's fresh-water springs in winter, the water's constant temperatures shielding them from the colder Gulf waters. Tour boats bring people to "swim with the manatees," although chasing or harassing them is illegal. Several small manatee sanctuaries have been established around King's Bay where humans are not allowed to enter. It is a delicate balance or tenuous compromise depending on one's perspective, one where human livelihoods and enjoyment are balanced against the safety and security of the manatees.

To view manatees from the vantage point of a boardwalk, visitors can take a trolley tour to the Three Sisters Springs National Wildlife Refuge in Crystal River and view a stunning concentration of manatees seeking refuge during cold spells. "You can tell the manatees that just came in from the Gulf because they still have barnacles on them," explained a volunteer ranger at Three Sisters Springs. "The barnacles usually drop off after about a week."

At Homosassa Springs State Park, one can climb down below the water level into "Nature's Giant Fishbowl" and see wild manatees and a huge concentration of salt and freshwater fish at eye level. There are also several captive animals in the park that have either been injured or born into captivity, so they cannot be released into the wild.

The actual coastline around Homosassa is largely pristine, being protected by the Chassahowitzka National Wildlife Refuge and Chassahowitzka Wildlife Management Area. Homosassa is generally thought to mean "a place where wild pepper grows," although other interpretations exist. The confusion lies in early attempts to spell out Native American words before a written alphabet was developed for the dialects, and there were no linguists making maps in the old days. The translation for Chassahowitzka is generally agreed upon to mean "hanging pumpkins" in the Muscogee language, one of two dialects used by Seminole Indians. The variety of pumpkins the Seminoles grew could climb trees, thus the name. The places—and their names—are all part of the enduring legacy of Florida's Nature Coast.

Moving slowly through these narrow inlets and channels of the island, with only the dense growth of mangrove, with its pendent rootlets, sprawling branches and evergreen foliage, one feels that he is lost in some seaside jungle of the tropics and not in that of a Florida key.

—W. S. BLATCHLEY, *MY NATURE NOOK,* 1931

4

MANGROVES, CULTURE, AND SUN

A mangrove forest can be an otherworldly type of place. From the outside, they appear to be thick green walls—impenetrable—with exposed tree roots that seem frozen in haphazard walking motions, like legions of soldiers marching in different directions. But upon closer examination, occasional openings in these mangrove jungles lead to long, canopied tunnels. Here, the sun's rays are filtered or blocked, and the air smells heavily of salt and decomposing vegetation. Birds call from a myriad of directions, and the curved mangrove branches often reveal flowering orchids and bromeliads, squirrel tree frogs, green anoles, mangrove tree crabs, and orange-brown mangrove salt marsh snakes. Life abounds in a mangrove forest!

If you head south along the Florida peninsula, Pinellas County just above Tampa Bay marks the beginning of extensive stretches of mangrove forests, even though this is a populous area that includes the cities of St. Petersburg, Clearwater, Largo, Tampa, Ruskin, Sarasota, and Bradenton. It is often called the Sun Coast, and beginning around Sarasota, the Cultural Coast, and one can explore undeveloped islands and peninsulas, historic sites, and points of interest, and the thick, jungle-like mangrove forests.

From the water, the first line of mangroves are dense green masses of trees with visible tangled roots that seem to be in motion. These are red mangroves, broad-leafed evergreen trees aptly named "walking trees" for the roots that prop them up as if frozen in

Visitors silhouetted against sunset at Honeymoon Island State Park.

The tangled prop roots of red mangroves, thus the name "walking trees."

stride. Not only are these trees attractive, but they are also the first line of defense against hurricanes, helping to absorb the tremendous wave action and winds associated with the storms.

Black mangroves grow at slightly higher elevations. These subtropical trees are distinguished by leaves with hairy undersides and roots with fingerlike projections, which provide oxygen to underwater roots. White mangroves are on even higher ground. They have no visible aerial root systems but are strongly rooted in the ground. White mangroves are easily identified by their leaves—yellow green in color and elliptical in shape, with two pimple-sized glands at the base of each stem. Of the more than 80 species of mangroves worldwide, only these three exist in Florida. The buttonwood tree, often found in mangrove forests, is considered a mangrove species by some scientists.

True Florida natives, the nearly 500,000 acres of mangrove forests in the Sunshine State are home to myriad sea life. The forests are ideal feeding and nursery grounds for fish—snapper, snook, tarpon, redfish, sheepshead, mullet, cobia, and more—up to 220 fish species!—as well as shrimp, oysters, and barnacles that cling to the plants' roots. The roots provide shelter from predators, and tree litter in the form of mangrove leaves, bark, and wood forms the base of a rich marine food source.

More than 180 bird species flock to Florida mangroves. In wading-bird rookeries, the thick green forests are alive with calls and cries of juvenile birds. Adults fly in and out on feeding runs and bicker with other birds over coveted branches.

Close-up of marsh or Harris hawk, one of many bird species that feed in mangroves.

Brown pelicans, great blue herons, brilliant white great egrets, stunning pink rose-ate spoonbills, and other species all perch, nest, and feed in the mangroves, as do ospreys, hawks, peregrine falcons, and bald eagles—the top echelon of aerial hunters fittingly occupying the topmost branches. Unique among them all is the mangrove cuckoo, whose extended range is Mexico, South America, and the Caribbean, but its only US habitat is the South Florida mangroves.

Because their many attributes are now largely recognized, mangroves have some degree of protection by Florida law and are faring better than in the past when developers destroyed vast forests. And there is evidence that mangroves are expanding their range as global temperatures warm, creeping north along both coasts. Researchers suggest this is not necessarily a good trend since mangroves are invading salt marsh habitats that are also valuable nursery grounds for a variety of marine creatures. Also, as sea level rises, mangroves will likely need to retreat inland but may end up being hemmed in by development. Another climate-related study found that the shade provided by mangroves is benefiting corals growing beneath them by reducing high levels of solar radiation, thus deterring coral bleaching that can kill corals.

Notable mangrove forests to explore along this stretch of coast include Caladesi Island State Park near Clearwater, Fort De Soto Park near Tierra Verde in Pinellas County, and the Weedon Island Preserve along the west side of Tampa Bay.

Besides mangroves, this stretch of coast is also known as the Cultural Coast, and one naturally thinks of Sarasota. The Florida land boom of 1925—and its collapse—played a large role in the area's evolution. Here's an alluring ad from

1925 for Whitfield Estates on Sarasota Bay: "Richest profits have come, since time began, to the man who pioneered—backed his vision with faith and action. You need only look about you; divide the staggering fortunes that bulge this country's banks. On the Florida west coast, now, you will find the pioneer blazing his trail through a land of wondrous beauty and fertile possibility—to assure profits in the years that are to come. Development has started and is striding steadily ahead, especially in this rich tropic country around Sarasota, where miles of productive back country ensure the continued prosperity and stability of this matchless home and play land."

When the land boom collapsed the following year, one man did follow through on a pioneering vision—John Ringling. Taking advantage of falling land prices, he purchased 150 acres and moved the Ringling Brothers and Barnum & Bailey Circus winter headquarters from Bridgeport, Connecticut, to Sarasota. His dream was to make the winter quarters more than a place to develop the next year's traveling show: "I'll build an open-air arena exactly the size of Madison Square Garden, and on Sunday the acts can practice before an audience. People will pay to watch the rehearsals—they'll think they're getting in on something special. Sarasota will become one of the most beautiful cities in Florida."

Soon, town residents were seeing disproportionately sized people, both small and large, along with women sporting beards in the grocery store aisles. And they started seeing tourists, lots of them. Sarasota quickly transformed from a small town to a major tourist destination. And even though the main circus company shut down for good in 2017, various types of circus arts and training still occur in Sarasota, and circus history is embedded throughout the community. Plus, the John and Mable Ringling Museum of Art, opened to the public in 1931, continues to draw crowds. Over time, it was combined with a circus museum, the historic Asolo Theater, an education center, the Bayfront Gardens, and the Ringlings' Ca' d'Zan Venetian gothic mansion. The entire complex is simply called The Ringling.

At The Ringling, visitors can marvel at European and American art masterpieces along with buildings that used red tile from Spain, slabs of delicate marble from Germany, veined marble from England, chandeliers and windows from Italy, and pecky cypress from the Sunshine State. The ornate gardens complement the buildings—stone walkways adorned with statues and colorful flowers dwarfed by tall palms and canopied by giant spreading banyan trees that grow ever larger with time.

History buffs can find other offerings along the Cultural Coast. Just south of Tampa Bay near Bradenton, the De Soto National Memorial marks the site where Hernando De Soto is believed to have landed with an army of soldiers, mercenaries, and clergy in 1539. From there, the Spaniards made their way through what is now the southeastern United States, fighting with indigenous people and spreading disease on a four-year, 4,000-mile odyssey that would change the "New World" forever and ultimately cost De Soto his life.

At the mouth of Tampa Bay sits the historic and strategic Egmont Key. A lighthouse was constructed on the island in 1848, the only one between St. Marks and Key West at the time, and it was tested that same September when a massive

The Venetian gothic Ca' d'Zan mansion of John and Mable Ringling in Sarasota.

hurricane sent a 15-foot storm surge across the island. An additional storm nearly toppled it, so Congress appropriated funds to reconstruct the lighthouse to "withstand any storm," and it still stands today, along with the keeper's house.

From 1855 to 1858, captured Seminoles from the Third Seminole War were confined to the island, and the Confederate army and then the Union navy occupied it during the Civil War. Fort Dade was built on the island in 1898 as part of the Spanish-American War, and it was active for 25 years. The Tampa Bay Pilots Association began operating on the island in 1926 to help guide vessels in and out of the bay, and they continue to operate today. The island is currently both a state park and national wildlife refuge, one that welcomes visitors only by boat to enjoy its historic structures and beaches. As sea level rises, Egmont Key is gradually becoming smaller, and the primary challenge is to protect its historic structures and unmarked graves of five Seminole Indians who died there, four of them children.

For Seminole Indians today, both in Florida and Oklahoma, Egmont Key represents the last Florida deportation center. One Seminole woman, Polly Parker, was placed on a ship for the west in 1858 only to escape at a refueling stop at St. Marks. She and a half dozen others walked all the way back to the Lake Okeechobee region, about 340 miles, and many of her descendants became prominent members of the tribe. So, besides a place of pain, Egmont Key represents resilience and pride to many Seminoles. "I don't know how she did it, but I am glad she did. Because, if she hadn't escaped, we would not be in Florida now," said tribal historian Willie Johns in a 2013 *Seminole Tribune* story. "Polly Parker's escape was a brave and

One of many gopher tortoises on Egmont Key in Tampa Bay.

defining moment in both Seminole and American history." Polly Parker lived to be more than 100 years old and died in 1921.

What does Egmont Key tell us about human history, from Tocabaga Indians to captured Seminoles to fortifications for wars that never came to our shores? With palm-draped brick walkways of a bygone era and vine-covered foundations of long-gone buildings, part of Egmont Key is Florida's version of a ghost town with shadows that perhaps have yet to see light. You get that feeling when walking the interior where something unseen seems to repel you from certain places, but not so much along its sunny shores where boaters and beachgoers play.

Egmont Key is a fascinating juxtaposition of history, natural beauty, and wild-life. Walk almost anywhere in the island's interior and a gopher tortoise or three can often be spotted. More than 1,000 gopher tortoises are found on the island. They seem to be everywhere. And one end of the island is closed to humans, a true sanctuary for shorebirds and other critters.

One can kayak or boat to Egmont Key or take the delightful Egmont Key Ferry out of Fort De Soto County Park. Boaters must be ever wary of Tampa Bay's sometimes busy shipping channel, 90 feet deep and often with waves that can accompany such an open water crossing.

Florida's cowboys also have roots in the Cultural Coast. Punta Rassa and Punta Gorda were the destinations for many a cattle drive in the late 1800s, whereupon the cows were paid for in Spanish gold and shipped to Cuba. For some early ranchers, it was a rags-to-riches story. There were wild scrub cattle for the taking— descendants of Spanish cattle released in the 1500s— and open range that could support a large number of grazing animals. Cattle were marked with distinctive brands or earmarks and rounded up by men who called themselves "cow hunters," otherwise known as "cracker cowboys" for the whips they cracked to drive cattle.

After the Indian wars of the West died down, Florida was considered an untamed "last frontier" and lured the famous western artist Frederic Remington to Punta Gorda in 1895. Remington, moaning the fencing of western rangeland, was sorely disappointed upon seeing Florida's open range cowboys. "Two very emaci-ated Texas ponies pattered down the street bearing wild-looking individuals whose hanging hair and drooping hats and generally bedraggled appearance would remind you at once of the Spanish moss which hangs so quietly and helplessly to the limbs of oaks out in the swamps," he wrote in *Harpers*. "The only thing they did which were conventional were to tie their ponies up by the head in brutal disregard, and then get drunk in about 15 minutes."

The cow hunter lived a rough life, often using a tin can for cooking, a saddle for a pillow, and smudge fires to discourage mosquitoes. Frequently, he had to deal with rattlesnakes and wild animals, and less frequently with floods and hurricanes. The Spanish longhorn cattle he hunted, marked, and tried to herd were often as wild as deer and not always cooperative. Once at their destination along the coast, many cow hunters blew most of their hard-earned pay on drink and fun. Shootings were commonplace, and storekeepers and bankers often wielded sawed-off shot-guns and had their places of business heavily fortified to deter looters. Eventually, more laws were enacted, the open rangelands of Florida started being fenced, and towns such as Punta Gorda began to prohibit "the running loose of horses, mules, jackasses, bulls, steers, cows, sheep, hogs or goats on town streets." The fun ended.

Historic house in Pass-a-Grille near the mouth of Tampa Bay.

Brown pelicans line the roof of Cortez Bait and Seafood.

Today, one is about as likely to catch a glimpse of Florida cowboys along the Sun Coast and Cultural Coast as they are in seeing a Florida black bear ambling along Clearwater Beach. The country's "last frontier" now has ample stretches of condominiums, shopping centers, chain businesses, and multilane highways, but historical communities such as Pass-a-Grille on a barrier island just west of St. Petersburg are where the pace slows. The skyline of buildings and tree-lined streets seem to blend more with the natural surroundings, the speed limit is slow, and one feels as though they have been transported back to an earlier era. Many residents are ever vigilant and oppose proposals for large motels and other developments that may threaten the town's historic nature, not wanting Pass-a-Grille to end up "like everywhere else." The town's name showed up as early as 1841 as *Passe-aux-Grilleurs*, so named by French fishermen using this point to cross over the island and stopping to grill their catch, although other versions of the name can be found.

Other historic seafaring communities include the fishing village of Cortez on Sarasota Bay and the traditional Greek sponge capital of Florida—Tarpon Springs. These communities feature generations-old buildings and interpretive exhibits and museums as well as people still following traditional lifestyles. They have adapted to changing times while standing strong against development proposals considered too drastic, such as high-rise condominiums.

A replica of an Aegean fishing village was how author Harnett T. Kane described Tarpon Springs in 1959. Kane added in *The Golden Coast*, "There are dark-eyed, strong-faced girls with the sturdiness of Mediterranean women; trim, mustachioed young men and older ones with shiny black hair and teeth whose whiteness seems whiter against well-burned skin. The fleet—once sailing, now motored vessels, broad-beamed and bright-hued—goes out about four times a year, to be away for many days as they labor on 'shares' under hard conditions. In a strange, blue-green, silent region they walk over coral gardens with balloon-like fish, tiny ones and monsters at their side, and danger present at every moment."

Author Ben Green, who has deep family roots in Cortez, wrote a tribute to his hometown in *Finest Kind* in 1985: "For a hundred years, the people of this small, unincorporated fishing village on the Gulf have lived a quiet life, earning a hard and honest living from the sea. But that way of life is threatened now by the twin plagues of the Florida coastline: high-rise condominiums and drug smugglers. . . . There are some who say it may already be too late. Others have given up. A few continue to fight." Today, the drug-running days are now colorful stories of the past, villagers have been largely successful fighting off condos, a few residents still fish for a living, and, according to one writer, "hungry, sleepy tourists are the new catch of the day."

The Osprey Trail in Honeymoon Island State Park features an increasingly rare old-growth slash pine forest.

The Cortez story is the classic Florida coast version of David versus Goliath where a small community stood up to big developers. There are no high rises here—only quaint houses, a few stores, and a post office. For visitors, there is a maritime museum of restored historic buildings, and along the waterfront, seafood restaurants thrive alongside seafood houses adorned with dozens of brown pelicans. The industry draws pelicans like squirrels to bird feeders, and perhaps the maritime native peoples had similar relationships. Some individual pelicans frequent certain docks and fishing piers so much that locals have given them names and speak of them fondly. To see so many brown pelicans is heartening when considering the bird was once on the verge of extinction.

Honeymoon Island in Pinellas County has a rich, romantic history, true to its name. A businessman named Clinton Washburn purchased the island in the late 1930s and came up with an idea of making the island a honeymoon retreat. He built 50 honeymoon cottages explicitly for honeymooners. He had 164 couples stay on the island until World War II cut his grand dream short. The island's cottages were then used for a retreat site for the employees of a Ohio defense contractor while the northern end of the island was used to test amphibious vehicles for use in the war. The cottages fell into disrepair after the war, and eventually a developer devised a plan to enlarge the 200-acre island to 3,000 acres by pumping in fill from the Gulf and building 4,500 residential houses along canals. The plan didn't go well since much of the fill was rock. The state of Florida eventually purchased the island and created Honeymoon Island State Park, now the state's busiest state park. A causeway connects the island to the mainland.

Besides beaches, Honeymoon Island State Park features the 2.5-mile Osprey Trail through an increasingly rare old-growth slash pine forest. The trail is aptly named since several osprey and their stick nests can be spotted. One might also hear or see great horned owls, marsh hawks, and other birds.

Only a few miles from Honeymoon Island, modern history is being made by the small coastal town of Dunedin. In early 2018, the state of Florida designated Dunedin as Florida's first trail town since the community has long been a mecca for nonmotorized paved trail users. Bicyclists, joggers, in-line skaters, and those enjoying a leisurely stroll can access the town by way of the Pinellas Trail, which runs through downtown on an abandoned CSX railroad corridor. The multiuse paved trail loop stretches from St. Petersburg to Tarpon Springs and loops back to St. Petersburg. The trail is credited with increasing Dunedin's business occupancy rate from 30 percent to 100 percent. Bike shops, cafés, motels, and other businesses cater to trail users.

"We couldn't be prouder," said Dunedin mayor Julie Ward Bujalski at the dedication. "Our downtown has thrived around the trail and attracted folks of all ages and abilities. We like to think of the trail as the main artery of our community."

Facing page: Dolphin statue and trail town banner in downtown Dunedin.

Starting in the 1980s, Dunedin embarked on a six-fold strategy to transform their town:

- Embrace the Pinellas Trail
- Foster adaptive reuse
- Slow traffic—pedestrian is #1
- Beautify, beautify, beautify!
- Build a sense of place
- Do small projects every year

From a town that resembled Anywhere USA in the 1970s with an overabundance of pavement and very few trees, Dunedin today is a landscaped and canopied gem with sidewalk cafes, quaint shops, a museum, and attractive waterfront, all within easy reach by foot or bicycle. It is a testament to communities that embrace the best of Florida's coast.

A couple watches the glow of a sunrise along the beach at Pass-a-Grille.

Land, water, and vegetation are just that dependent on one another. Without these primary elements in natural balance, we can have neither fish nor game, wildflowers nor trees, labor nor capital, nor sustaining habitat for humans.

—JAY NORWOOD "DING" DARLING

Calusa Indian exhibit at the Florida Museum of Natural History in Gainesville.

5

CALUSA WHISPERS

How did early native people and the Paleo people before them describe the Florida coast in their many dialects? What did they call the different islands and passes, capes and shores? What about favorite fishing and shell fishing spots or different winds and clouds, storms and hurricanes? What did they call the various fish, birds, manatee, dolphin, and myriad sea creatures? And what about currents, waves, water depths, shades of blue water, or striking sunrises and sunsets? What kind of adventures did they share around evening fires? Each tribal generation certainly had talented storytellers and artists to interpret the coastal environment, but we only have a speck of what they produced over millennia, most of which were found in the peat of Marco Island.

In 1896, Marco Island, then called Key Marco, yielded some of the most astounding Native American artifacts ever found in Florida. Digging in the island's mangrove muck, Frank Hamilton Cushing and his Smithsonian expedition crew uncovered an incredible array of perishable objects—elaborately carved and painted wood animal heads, masks, clubs, bowls, and *atlatls* (spear-throwing devices). They also found nets, fishhooks, cord, ropes, floats, and shell jewelry. Cushing later wrote of these early people, "their art is not only an art of the sea, but is an art of shells and teeth, an art for which the sea supplied nearly all the working parts of tools, the land only some of the materials worked upon."

South Florida's Calusa Indians had a creative side as indicated by the Key Marco artifacts. A painted wooden alligator head and a wooden cat figure with human-like legs were among the items found. They did not rely heavily on pottery. Instead, they were also known as "the Shell Indians" because they used shells for tools, spear points, jewelry, and ornaments. They dug long canals, built huge shell mounds, and erected palm-roofed structures on stilts. Not surprisingly, they were also mariners who frequently sailed large dugout canoes to Cuba and up and down the west coast, dominating nearby tribes.

The Calusa settled along the coast as far back as 2,500 years ago. The first European visitor was believed to be Juan Ponce de Leon in 1513. De Leon is said to have named the larger of the two barrier islands "San Ybel"—later called Sani-bel—after Queen Isabella of Spain. The Spanish explorer often battled with the Calusa Indians and eventually died from a Calusa arrow wound during a second visit to the region in 1521. The Calusa, labeled "the fierce people" by the Span-ish, prevented the Spanish from establishing any kind of permanent colony on the islands for 200 years, but by the late 1700s, most of the Calusa had died from European-introduced diseases or had fallen prey to English-sponsored slave raid-ers. Many Calusa survivors went to Cuba with the Spanish, although it is believed that some Calusa descendants stayed in Florida and eventually joined the Seminole resistance. The Seminole band that raided Indian Key in 1840 is believed to have included Calusa descendants.

The Calusa believed there were three superior beings that, in turn, controlled the weather, the tribe's welfare, and warfare. Also, each person had three souls: in the eye's pupil, reflection in the water, and in one's shadow. Only the soul in the eye's pupil remained with the body after death, and this is the one relatives could communicate with at the grave site. The other souls migrated through animals, each animal becoming successively smaller until the souls dissolved into nothingness.

Today, one can touch the Calusa people by visiting Mound Key in Estero Bay, believed to be the ceremonial center of the Calusa kingdom and where Calusa leader King Carlos likely lived in the 1500s. Compared to the surrounding man-grove forests, the 30-foot mound is a mountain, and the view from the summit is impressive. Standing atop the mound where so many Calusa once stood provides perspective. Nothing remains of the massive Calusa village here except for this mound of shells, an entire 2,500-year-old civilization gone. This beacon from the past begs to ask the question: what will we leave behind for future generations to behold and ponder?

Another important Calusa site is the Randell Research Center on Pine Island where a Calusa-built mound and canal can be seen along with a small museum. It is all part of the rich history and bounty known today as the Paradise Coast.

Seminole Indians also used the Southwest Florida coast, but primarily for trade. Before and during the Second Seminole War, they traded cattle and other goods with ships from Spanish Cuba in exchange for arms, ammunition, and gunpowder.

Group climbing Mound Key in Estero Bay, once believed to be the ceremonial center of the Calusa kingdom.

The Spanish rifles were considered excellent weaponry when compared to the flintlock muzzle-loading muskets that many American soldiers used at the time.

The same thing that inspired the Calusa to live along the Gulf—an incredible abundance and variety of fish and marine resources—initially brought Cuban fishermen, mostly in the spring and fall. They learned how to net fish from the Calusa and built large palm-thatched huts, using hammocks for sleeping. Outside were pit fires for cooking and bug defense along with wood racks for drying and salting fish, fish that was often shipped back to Cuba to feed a growing population of enslaved Indian and African workers.

New England fishermen began venturing into Florida waters in the mid-to-late 1800s. They soon learned that ice was a key ingredient to keep deep water fish such as grouper and red snapper from spoiling. Oyster industries and then shrimp trawling followed, but what really drew anglers to southwest Florida in large numbers wasn't food fish or shellfish at all. It was sportfishing. And no fish filled that niche like the tarpon. Nicknamed "the silver king," tarpon can grow more than 8 feet in length and weigh up to 280 pounds, often living more than 50 years. When an angler hooks his or her first tarpon, witnessing acrobatic midair vaults as the drag on the reel screams, they are often hooked on the sport for life. And because tarpon come into shallower bays and inlets in the spring and summer, they are much more accessible than deep-sea fish.

Tarpon fishing began in the 1890s and continues today as a largely catch-and-release fish. The state's most famous tarpon fishing waters is Boca Grande Pass, one of Florida's deepest at up to 80 feet. The pass connects the Gulf to Charlotte Harbor, a rich body that receives both the Peace and Myakka Rivers and where tarpon and other fish spawn in May and June. "Tarpon fishing is a cross between hunting elephants, searching for whale and picking up a live wire," concluded author Karl A. Bickel in his 1942 book *The Mangrove Coast.* "Sometimes you will spot them—fifty or a hundred of them—madly thrashing about in circles, their tails flashing in the sun like propeller blades, the water churned foamy. . . . At times when there will be hundreds of tarpon exploding about you boiling up in clusters on all sides, not a fish will be taken. Then suddenly the fish will bite! . . . The instant the tarpon feels the hook the battle is on. There are few feeble fighters. The big silversides will be in the air with a smashing rush, the water will fall away in waves as he comes up, his head shaking madly to throw off the hook. Three—four—five times he will make the leap and then will probably sound deeply and see-saw all the way up. An average weight for a tarpon is around sixty-five pounds and a sixty-five pounder can keep a fisherman in a state of nervous hysteria for twenty-five minutes without exerting himself at all."

Writer Wallace Stevens called the Gulf "the fishy sea" due to the incredible diversity and abundance of fish, but for the angler, nothing compares to the fighting tarpon in terms of pure exhilaration.

Unfortunately, this section of coast and other parts of the Southwest Florida coastline has had to contend with near annual outbreaks of red tide in recent years. Red tide is a naturally occurring microscopic algae that releases something known as brevetoxins that can kill fish and other marine life and irritate the eyes, nose, throat, and lungs of human residents and visitors. Understandably, red tide has a dampening effect on tourism and fishing in the region, so scientists and community leaders are looking at ways to minimize red tide and its effects, often netting and cleaning up dead fish in the waters and on beaches on a frequent basis. Some scientists speculate that warmer Gulf temperatures along with excess nutrients from fertilizers and runoff, including massive releases from Lake Ockeechobee, can worsen red tide outbreaks.

"People need to get involved," said charter fishing captain Ozzie Lessinger in a 2021 news report. "They need to understand that the lifeblood of our community for probably 60 to 80 percent of the businesses is water quality and if we don't fight for that water quality. . . we will lose it."

Besides fishing, this section of coast offers its share of charm and natural beauty, highlighted by its islands. There are publicly owned jewels only reachable by boat such as Cayo Costa State Park and private islands such as Cabbage Key where one can have a "Cheeseburger in Paradise" at the Cabbage Key Inn Restaurant, the place where locals say Jimmy Buffett was inspired to write his hit song. More developed islands are connected to the mainland by causeways and bridges. Sanibel and Captiva Islands—linked together by a short bridge—are where stores,

Sanibel Island has strict ordinances limiting the size of signs and the height of buildings, and multiuse paths are common.

restaurants, motels, and houses have been developed in such a tasteful manner that one begins to wish all of Florida's growth could have been guided in such a way.

Shelling is world famous on Sanibel, and a humorous term has been coined for beach ramblers searching for shells, "the Sanibel stoop." Not surprising, the Bailey-Matthews National Shell Museum is housed on the island, the only nationally accredited museum in the country solely devoted to shells and mollusks. Besides shells, some beachcombers also seek out sea beans—the seeds of tropical plants—that can float on ocean currents for years and decades. They are often colorful and of different shapes and sizes, and, like shells, some are rare. Most of what is found on Sanibel are called sea pearls, while a larger variety of sea beans are found along the Atlantic coast. Collecting sea glass is another beachcombing hobby; the rarest examples of these tumbled and rounded pieces of colorful glass come from old shipwrecks.

There is something relaxing about shelling and beachcombing. It's simple. You scan the beach and tidal wrack or wade into the water while searching the bottom and pick up beautiful creations of nature. People who lead highly technical lives are quickly reduced to hunter-gatherers, and stress just sheds off like the husks of shells being sought. On Sanibel beach, I helped a couple from London who were intent on finding a starfish to show their 10-month-old daughter. Appropriately, I found a young starfish in the surf about 4 inches long and called them over. We held it up, and the infant touched it with tentative fingers—her five fingers almost the size

Sea dollar and whelk shell along the surf of Sanibel Island.

of the starfish with its five appendages. Her look was one of innocent wonderment. A simple moment, a gentle moment, found on the beach of Sanibel.

Early history was not so gentle. The pirate Jose Gaspar used the islands as a base in the early 1800s. He built a prison for female captives that he held for ransom on the "Isle de los Captivas," later called Captiva Island, and he is rumored to have buried stolen treasure on Sanibel Island, although no one claims to have found it.

Seminole Indians scared away settlers in the early 1800s, and it was only after the Civil War when pioneers began to establish themselves. A lighthouse was built on Sanibel Island in 1884 to guide mariners, and in the late 1880s, the first resort was built, the Sisters (later named the Casa Ybel). By 1892, almost 100 people lived on Sanibel and Captiva Islands. Over time, several well-known people frequented the islands, including Thomas Edison, Henry Ford, President Theodore Roosevelt, the poet Edna St. Vincent Millay, and Charles and Anne Morrow Lindbergh. Anne Morrow Lindbergh's *Gift from the Sea* is still a treasured classic, in which she often mixed ocean metaphors with life's lessons. "The sea does not reward those who are too anxious, too greedy, or too impatient," she wrote. "To dig for treasures shows not only impatience and greed, but lack of faith. Patience, patience, patience, is what the sea teaches. Patience and faith. One should lie empty, open, choiceless as a beach—waiting for a gift from the sea."

One person who had a tremendous impact on the islands was a prize-winning political cartoonist and wildlife conservation leader named Jay Norwood "Ding" Darling. Darling initiated efforts to purchase and restore wetlands, having started the federal Duck Stamp Program. He often spent winters on Captiva Island and

White pelicans wintering in the J.N. "Ding" Darling National Wildlife Refuge.

The colorful, yellow-crowned night heron is one of many birds that frequent the J.N. "Ding" Darling National Wildlife Refuge.

Shells spill out of a Calusa Indian shell midden on Sanibel Island in the J.N. "Ding" Darling National Wildlife Refuge.

sought federal protection of Sanibel and Captiva's fragile ecosystem. The J.N. "Ding" Darling National Wildlife Refuge was established in 1945, protecting more than 6,400 acres and providing habitat to more than 245 species of birds and numerous mammals, reptiles, and amphibians.

Today, the "Ding" Darling Refuge is one of the greatest bird-watching hotspots in North America. Along the 4-mile Wildlife Drive that people bike as much as drive, visitors often speak in hushed tones at the viewing spots so as not to spook the birds or break the spell. In some of the larger tidal pools or lakes ringed by mangroves, hundreds of wading birds are spread out in all directions, often gleaming like cotton bolls since most have white plumage. In winter, white pelicans astound visitors with their size, especially when standing on sandbars since adults are 5 feet tall with a wingspan of more than 8 feet. They are often found in clusters while more solitary are the black and yellow-crowned night herons, striking in their quiet beauty.

Wildlife Drive is open every day of the week except Friday, so the birds have at least one day of privacy without the prying eyes of humans with their binoculars, spotting scopes, and zoom lenses. Not surprisingly, Calusa shell middens can also be found in the refuge, easily seen along an interpretive trail. "In the final analysis, an Islander is not just a permanent Sanibel resident," wrote Margaret Greenberg in *Nature on Sanibel*. "Rather, a true Islander is *anyone* who loves the island and wants to retain the delicate balance between its two major attractions: vacation haven and wildlife sanctuary."

After a causeway from the mainland was built in 1963, residents worried that development, if uncontrolled, would ruin the island. Interestingly, several former CIA operatives retired to Sanibel in the early 1970s, and they started a newspaper and helped residents incorporate and form a city government so they could fight pro-development county leaders at the time. Sanibel's first elected mayor—ex-spy Porter Goss—went on to serve in Congress as chairman of the House Intelligence Committee and two years as CIA director. "The CIA recruits leaders, and they train you to lead," Goss explained in a 1987 *Miami Herald* article.

Island land-use restrictions were enacted in 1974 to temper growth and restrict such things as tree cutting, building heights, and signs. Even the 7-Eleven has a modest sign, perhaps the smallest in the country for this chain. Most of the stores and restaurants are locally owned, and like most of Florida's coast, there are favorite seafood restaurants where music thumps, seafood is fresh, and libations flow freely. One restaurant is Doc Ford's, inspired by Randy Wayne White's Doc Ford detective novels. With an island full of ex-CIA operatives, White had plenty of material to draw from.

Sanibel and Captiva Islands have become a model for coastal growth management in the state, and most visitors and residents feel the charm and natural beauty of the islands have been preserved alongside vestiges of its historical past, including the once powerful Calusa Indian culture.

Gulls and terns rest along a beach on Sanibel Island.

6

EVERGLADES WILDERNESS

View of the Everglades River of Grass from the Shark Valley tower.

When Florida's coast dips into the remote Ten Thousand Islands, the white sandy beaches end, and a maze of undeveloped islands and tidal creeks begin. It is a world unto its own. Once serving as a refuge for Seminole Indians followed by recluses and outlaws, the Ten Thousand Islands and Everglades are now havens for wilderness lovers, and there is a rich history to explore.

Historic landmarks remain, such as Chokoloskee's Smallwood Store where proprietor Ted Smallwood once traded with dugout-paddling Seminole Indians. The Indians swapped pelts and silver money for tools, guns, and staples. The store is now a museum, seemingly frozen in an earlier time, and the vast watery wilderness of islands, sawgrass, mangroves, forests, waterways, and open water of the coastal Everglades and Ten Thousand Islands appears little different than when dugout travelers fished the waters and set up villages and camps on the islands. The name Chokoloskee means "old house" in the Seminole-Creek tongue, so the large island was surely used by Seminoles before the first white settlers arrived in the 1870s.

Before the Seminoles, Calusa Indians are believed to have reached down into these parts and dug canals and built up and even created some of the islands. And because most of the land and waters in this vast wilderness are now protected by Everglades National Park, visitors arrive from throughout the United States and the world.

Below Sanibel and Everglades City in the region of the Shark the great wall of mangrove, made up of amazing trees, sometimes passing eighty feet in height, something to be seen nowhere else in all the world, form a deep green palisade along the shore. Behind it lie the mysterious depths of the Florida Labyrinth which has yet to be fully explored.

—KARL A. BICKEL, *THE MANGROVE COAST*, 1942

The saga of how the glades got drained and its connection to Indian wars, railroaders, road builders, outlaws, land hucksters, sugar oligarchs, battles over conservation and panther survival is a story as lusty as anything ever imagined about America.

—HERB HILLER, *SOUTH FLORIDA SUN SENTINEL*, 2003

Inside Smallwood Store Museum in Chokoloskee.

An Everglades alligator in Shark Valley opens its mouth to cool itself.

On foot, one can hike through the Big Cypress National Preserve on the Florida National Scenic Trail. The 1,500-mile footpath begins at the Oasis Visitor Center on the Tamiami Trail, and most hikers take to the trail during the dry season from November through April, and even then, it can still be wet. This type of exploration can have its rewards, especially for those seeking solitude and a true feeling of wilderness. One might even see signs—or a glimpse—of the rare Florida panther since Big Cypress sits in the heart of its remaining stronghold.

Regarding the Everglades' famous 60-mile-wide and 100-mile-long "River of Grass," the easiest way to experience it is to visit Shark Valley. You won't see any sharks, and it's not a valley in the traditional sense with mountains or cliffs on either side. Shark Valley is a barely perceptible shallow depression that feeds the Shark River, and as the Shark River nears the coast, bull sharks can be found there, thus the name. A paved and usually dry 15-mile loop trail enables visitors to hike, bike, or take a guided tram tour through Shark Valley. Numerous wading birds, osprey, and alligators are all but guaranteed to be seen, and a highlight is a three-story viewing tower halfway around the loop. The view of sawgrass marsh and tree islands is expansive, and it's all part of the slow-moving freshwater "river" flowing into Florida Bay and Gulf of Mexico at an average rate of 100 feet per day, as described in 1947 by Marjory Stoneman Douglas in *The Everglades: River of Grass*: "The miracle of the light pours over the green and brown expanse of saw grass and of water, shining and slow-moving below, the grass and water that is the meaning and the central fact of the Everglades of Florida. It is a river of grass."

Another way to explore the Everglades wilderness is to paddle a canoe or kayak in the same spirit as early Native Americans and Seminole Indians. Paddlers can observe a unique combination of subtropical and tropical plants, creatures from marine and estuarine environments, and both alligators and crocodiles since this is the only place in the world where the two reptiles coexist. Bird life includes bright pink roseate spoonbills, soaring ospreys, white pelicans, and wood storks. Sea turtles can often be seen poking up their heads in the Gulf and Florida Bay. If fortunate, a paddler might glimpse a rare sawfish. Its long, flat snout contains 24 or more pairs of sharp teeth that resemble a two-bladed crosscut saw.

Paddlers have two main choices for long-distance trips. The 99-mile Wilderness Waterway between Everglades City and Flamingo follows a series of tidal rivers, streams, and lakes until emptying into Florida Bay around Cape Sable. The other route is along the edge of the Gulf and Florida Bay, with campsites mostly on undeveloped islands. Both are part of the statewide Florida Circumnavigational Saltwater Paddling Trail.

Along the Gulf islands route, bugs tend to be less bothersome since breezes are more prevalent, although raccoons have even been known to chew through thin plastic water jugs to retrieve fresh water, especially during dry periods. Paddlers doing either route must bring enough fresh water for seven to eight days—and they should guard it well.

Paddling either the Wilderness Waterway or the coastal islands route can be challenging, especially if encountering swarms of mosquitoes, strong winds, thunderstorms, and adverse tides. You can better appreciate what Native Americans and pioneers endured while living or traveling through the region, and why Seminole Indians and outlaws once sought refuge along the sometimes bewildering, twisting waterways. As Nevin O. Winter wrote in 1918, "Down in the mazes of the Ten Thousand Islands, one will sometimes meet men who turn their faces away and will merely smile if you ask them their names. Sometimes they kill men whom they fear are after them, and occasionally they slay each other either in a drunken quarrel or for the purpose of robbery."

Many Everglades residents followed an unwritten code: Suspect every man; ask no questions; settle your own quarrels; never steal from an islander; stick by him, even if you do not know him; shoot quick, when your secret is in danger; and cover your kill.

The most infamous outlaw of the region was Ed Watson, immortalized by Peter Matthiessen in his trilogy of novels, *Killing Mr. Watson*, *Lost Man's River*, and *Bone by Bone*. A beast of a man with an enormous red beard, "Emperor Watson," as he was sometimes called due to the wealth he accumulated, had allegedly killed Belle Starr in Oklahoma and a man in Arcadia before calling the Ten Thousand Islands home in the early 1880s. He continued to have various run-ins with the law for attempted murder and alleged murder—trouble just seemed to show up wherever he went.

As described in my book *Wild Florida Waters*, Watson had a habit of hiring people and not paying them at his farm on a chunk of uplands called Chatham Bend Key that he had purchased from a widow of another outlaw. When the crops

were all in, cords of buttonwood had been gathered, and cane juice had been squeezed, boiled down into syrup, and packed in tins, the workers demanded pay. At this point, Watson thought it best to offer early retirement by knife or gun rather than part with scarce cash. It was a business decision. A new crew—usually consisting of transient men with few family ties and some who were wanted by the law—could easily be hired the next season. Numerous graves were later uncovered. Many other victims likely lay at the bottom of the swamps and Florida Bay.

Finally, in fall 1910, the fine citizens of Chokoloskee had had enough. They were tolerant of moonshining, smuggling, hunting birds for their plumes, and other illegal activities. And if a man wanted to hide out from the law in the remote maze of islands, creeks, and swamps like the Seminoles once did, that was fine—no questions asked—as long as they didn't murder folks for no good reason. Enough was

Sunrise at a canoe/kayak camp in the Ten Thousand Islands where paddlers can choose from a number of islands for camping on short- or long-distance trips.

enough. So, when Watson tied up his boat at the town's boat landing, a crowd gathered, and Watson was publicly accused of killing another of his hands. They demanded his gun. Watson's short temper flared. He raised his shotgun and pressed the trigger.

Unknowingly, Watson had purchased water-damaged shells from Smallwood Store in Chokoloskee a few days before, so the gun misfired. The crowd, using good shells, then opened fire. It was as clean a community execution as you'll find in Florida's history. One witness observed he had never seen a man so dead. Watson's body was buried on Rabbit Key, but it was later moved to Ft. Myers to rest alongside his wife's grave. No need to lure trouble from the afterlife.

The stories didn't end there. After Watson, the infamous mobster Al Capone is believed to have run a huge moonshining operation deep in the Everglades in the 1930s. The Lost City, also known as "Ghost Village," allegedly supplied spirits to a nearby saloon and dance hall. It was also the site of a Native American village and a place where Confederate soldiers might have hidden out after stealing Union gold during the Civil War. Stories are thick, but facts are sketchy, similar to tales of the elusive skunk ape some say lurk in the great swamp. The official Skunk Ape Headquarters sits along the Tamiami Trail in tiny Ochopee, also the site of the smallest post office building in the United States.

Historically, residents of the region have had a gift for tale telling, such as Panther Key's Juan Gomez, affectionately called Old John by those who knew him. Born in the 1770s, Gomez claimed to have met Napoleon, served with the pirate Jose Gaspar (Gasparilla), fought in the Second Seminole War, and operated as a blockade runner during the Civil War. He named his home Panther Key because panthers would swim to the island and eat his goats. Juan Gomez attracted many visitors and writers to Panther Key, and one visitor in 1898 mentioned that Gomez had a young wife and that at age 120, Gomez was surprisingly vigorous: "his complexion was brown, dark and rich [in] color as century old mahogany; his thick white hair, bushy and plentiful, framed a face seamed and lined but keen and full of vigor." Gomez died in 1900 at age 122. Some say he had been the oldest person in the United States.

While human history is highly colorful in the Everglades region, most of the waterways and islands belong to nature. More than 360 species of birds have been spotted in these unique southwest Florida habitats. Numerous fish, dolphins, and manatees frequent the channels, bays, and coves of the area. Rich seagrass beds are nursery grounds for a variety of fish, shellfish, and crustaceans, and they also provide food for manatees and sea turtles.

Unfortunately, to the detriment of many native creatures in the Everglades and Florida Bay and the people who depend on them, pumps, floodgates, and retention ponds outside the park now largely control the Everglades' lifegiving fresh water supply. A multibillion-dollar restoration plan is hopefully fixing some of the problems, along with improved timing of water releases.

Everglades City is a gateway to the Ten Thousand Islands and an important hub for several paddling trails, including the 1,515-mile Florida Circumnavigational Saltwater Paddling Trail. The town is also bike friendly, as evidenced by bicycle racks throughout town and at the airport. "What struck me about Everglades City was the level of community involvement," said Katie Bernier, South Regional Trails coordinator for the Florida Office of Greenways and Trails. "This is an area that was heavily impacted by Hurricane Irma, but residents have since worked tirelessly in restoring their town, keeping recreational opportunities their primary focus."

Local historian and avid bicyclist Patty Huff spearheaded successful efforts for Everglades City to become a state-designated trail town, and she enjoys showing off the charm and history of the town to visitors. "We are one of the few coastal towns that still has buildings that go back a hundred years," she said. "I love living in a town that has an historic and cultural nature. A lot of coastal towns don't have that."

The city hall of Everglades City built by Barron Collier in the 1920s.

Steve and Patty Huff in their historic home in Everglades City.

The Everglades City Rod and Gun Club, which features a large public restaurant and bar, was built on the foundation of the first permanent white settlement in 1864, and the interior has changed little since Victorian times. There are vintage cash registers, oil paintings, furniture, light fixtures, and, of course, numerous fish and wildlife mounts.

Most of Everglades City was laid out and built in 1923 by American advertising entrepreneur Barron Gift Collier, who was the largest landowner in Florida at the time. Inspired by city designs around the world, Collier did not hold back. He built a four-lane avenue called Broadway, installed an electric streetcar, and put in a cage of rhesus monkeys to entertain the children. The town hall and other buildings were built of concrete and stucco in the Classical Revival style popular in France and Italy. Collier even printed his own currency or "scrip" that could only be used in Collier establishments.

The town was called Everglades then, but the name was eventually expanded to Everglades City. It became the county seat for the legislatively established Collier County after Collier agreed to finish the western half of the Tamiami Trail. Everglades City was used as a base for building the Tamiami Trail, completed in 1928. The Tamiami Trail allowed visitors to drive to Everglades City from either Naples or Miami rather than travel by boat.

"What nature failed to supply, his [Collier's] imagination, vision, managerial skill, and, above all, his capital, would soon provide," wrote historian Charlton Tebeau in *Florida's Last Frontier: The History of Collier County*. "The new Everglades [City] first took form in the mind of this man who had set out to develop the county to which he gave his name, and most of which he owned." But if Collier had big city dreams for Everglades City, it never materialized. The town's population peaked in 1950 at 625 residents.

Patty and her husband Steve, a renowned fishing guide, fell in love with the rich history of Everglades City, transplanting from the Florida Keys in 1994. They restored a beautiful historic home in the heart of downtown, built around 1920. Among Patty's many projects is to raise funds to restore the town's century-old bank building and turn it into a trail town headquarters and Everglades area welcome center. One favorite story told about the bank is when floodwaters from Hurricane Donna in 1960 soaked all the paper money and mortgage papers. Bank tellers hung the bills and papers on clotheslines in the sun and, when dry, nothing turned up missing!

Current employment in Everglades City centers on stone crab fishing, recreational fishing, airboat tours, and kayak and canoe outfitting. It wasn't always the case. Smuggling "square grouper" through the maze of the Ten Thousand Islands in small boats was big during the 1970s and early 1980s, and stories still abound. "My daddy used to fill up his trailer with marijuana from smuggling boats," a fishing guide told me. "He was paid in stacks of bills. The hundreds were in stacks of a thousand dollars and there were big rolls of fives, tens, and twenties. He would give me all the fives, and my whole top dresser drawer was full of fives all through

Sunset strollers in Everglades City along the Barron River.

high school." Eventually, most involved in the smuggling were caught because someone "ratted them out" and the high times were over.

Sunset along the Barron River on the western edge of Everglades City is a great place to meet local residents where talk is usually of fishing, local high school sports, and weather. One couple even walks their parrot with a wheeled perch. It is a slow, relaxed pace, with the nearest city being 36 miles away. One can also enjoy a free ping-pong game at the local Marathon station. A table is set up between the two gas pumps. "It was my son's idea, and people love it," explained the manager with a smile, and it was obvious she didn't want to discourage youthful entrepreneurship.

If traveling along the Everglades coast toward Flamingo by watercraft, one memorable spot is Cape Sable, one of the finest natural shorelines remaining in Florida. A grassy plain borders the sandy beach in most places, with occasional clumps of sable palms, Jamaica dogwood, and hardwood hammocks. Gopher tortoises and Cape Sable seaside sparrows are among the protected species here, with the Cape Sable seaside sparrow being the only bird restricted entirely to the Everglades environment. They depend upon prairies that both periodically flood and burn.

Before the national park was established in 1947, many attempts to farm, ranch, and develop Cape Sable were short-lived due to its remoteness, insect life, and killer hurricanes.

A ping-pong table sits ready for players between gas pumps at the Marathon station in Everglades City.

If traveling the more interior route to Flamingo, one can camp at Watson's Place at Chatham Bend Key, site of Ed Watson's infamous abode. Some say the place is haunted.

The tiny town of Flamingo anchors the eastern edge of the Everglades shore. By land, it is 48 miles from Homestead, and many drive the distance because destinations at the end of a road simply have a certain attraction.

Flamingo, named in 1893 for the colorful birds that once arrived in great numbers from Cuba and the Bahamas, was never more than a handful of rustic houses, most built on pilings. It had no Barron Collier as a visionary patriarch. Mosquitoes were and are infamous in Flamingo, so thick that one naturalist in 1893 reported that a swarm extinguished an oil lamp. Before air conditioning, interior walls of buildings were described as being thickly sooted from constantly burning smudge pots to keep mosquitoes at bay. Even baby carriages were said to have smoldering smudge pots underneath.

Most early residents fished, grew sugar cane, cut buttonwood for charcoal, hunted wading birds for the plume trade, or made moonshine. Area moonshine was labeled "Cape Sable Augerdent," a brew so powerful that it brought tears to some users. "I thought I had been drinking carbolic acid," testified one visitor.

When a scarcely navigable road was built to Flamingo in 1922, one resident quipped, "There were fewer people than ever at Flamingo. They had found a way to get out."

Of course, Flamingo is perched on the northern edge of Florida Bay, one that links the Everglades to the Florida Keys and Cuba. At 850 square miles in size,

Florida Bay is the largest estuary in Florida. Yet, the bay averages only 3 feet in depth. A basketball center could wade its entire length without getting his head wet. In this way, Florida Bay is similar to the shallow Everglades "river of grass" just to the north, and it is just as endangered. Like the Everglades, Florida Bay has been starved of vital freshwater, and freshwater often flows in at the wrong time of year to reap the best benefit for spawning fish and wading birds. And like the Everglades, Florida Bay is dependent upon extensive efforts to both increase and cleanse incoming freshwater sources and to restore the historic timing of freshwater flows.

When visiting Florida Bay along the shore at Flamingo, one can easily give way to blissful ignorance of its challenges. There are egrets and white herons, willets, and black-necked stilts, all poking along the water's edge. American crocodiles swim just offshore, and fins of predatory fish slice through the water. Mullet leap. Osprey peep, and the unmistakable whistle of a bald eagle cuts through the air, as it swoops down from a bleached, storm-battered tree. No wonder Seminole and Miccosukee Indians fought so tenaciously to stay in their Everglades home, and to be left alone.

Why save Florida Bay and the Everglades? Its animal residents can give you a thousand reasons, and its wilderness nature is a lure many find hard to resist.

Regal-looking pelican at sunset sits on a dock post in the Ten Thousand Islands.

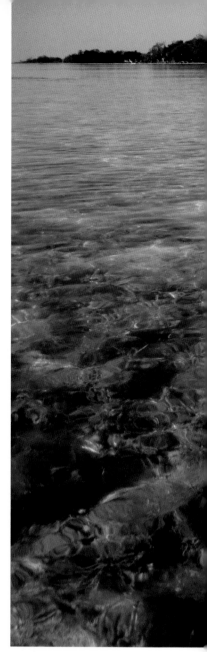

7

THE KEYS: A PLACE LIKE NO OTHER

Watching a sunset is a ritual anywhere along the Gulf Coast since the shore faces west or southwest, but sunset watching has developed into an art form at Mallory Square in Key West. Mark Twain, Tennessee Williams, and many other iconic figures partook in the celebration, one that now includes musicians, jugglers, clowns, psychics, magicians, and food vendors, much like a medieval fair. It's a combination of festive culture and natural beauty, and troubles of the day seem to melt with the red orb that sinks into the waves. "The myriad performers and beautiful scenery make this a once-in-a-lifetime experience," wrote one satisfied visitor in an online review.

The street performers come and go as they sometimes travel to other cities around the world. In 2021, the performer who drew the largest crowd was Jean Morabal, also known as Blue. In his late 20s, Blue learned juggling in middle school and has been performing for tips since. He starts out with both feet on the ground while juggling large swords, but then he hops on an 8-foot unicycle with some assistance and juggles flaming batons as the dipping sun illuminates his form in flaming orange and red hues. The crowd shows its appreciation by filling his hat with paper money. But it is the sunset itself that receives the loudest ovation at Mallory Square. Mother Nature still puts on the best show, although no one throws dollars into the water for a tip. And as the color fades, the crowd quiets

Clear waters in the Florida Keys reveal a bright orange-red Bahama starfish.

The region of the Keys is one of ever-shifting beauty, of seas and greenery of many shadings, of great clouds and drifting flowers. When John James Audubon saw it he cried out in admiration of the wild expanse, of great pink birds such as he had met nowhere else. Others have stared in wonder at the flying fish, the iridescent creatures of many hues, tiny, exotic ones and near-monsters of the waters in which the Gulf and the Atlantic have their meeting.

—HARNETT T. KANE, *THE GOLDEN COAST*, 1959

This contemporary view of Key West is reminiscent of historic times.

Jean Morabal, otherwise known as Blue, performs at the Mallory Square sunset ceremony.

Chickens roam freely in downtown Key West.

momentarily as if showing respect before dispersing for the many bars, restaurants, and live music venues in downtown Key West.

In many ways, the 1938 words of Stockbridge and Perry, two authors who wrote *So This Is Florida*, still ring true: "Key West has an exotic charm which lures one who has once visited this ancient stronghold of Caribbean pirates irresistibly back again."

In the Florida Keys, a stretch of coast needing no other name, visitors also enjoy crystalline waters, coral reefs, mangrove tunnels, and a fun-loving maritime culture. Regarding the natural world, observant visitors can peel back layer upon layer of biological diversity. Take, for example, the number of different marine species found in the Florida Keys National Marine Sanctuary, which is all of the Keys and Dry Tortugas—a total of roughly 6,000. Let that sink in for a moment. Six thousand unique species of marine life ranging from manatees and sea turtles to lobsters, fish, eels, and stingrays. Part of this is due to the long stretch of living reefs along the Keys and extending up the Southeast Coast, with Florida being the only state in the continental United States with a living reef tract. The state boasts 300 miles of coral reefs, the third-largest barrier reef system in the world, although coral bleaching, pollution, and ocean acidification are challenging the health of reef ecosystems. Besides ecosystem benefits, healthy coral reefs can absorb 97 percent of wave energy from storms and hurricanes, thereby protecting people, property, and habitat for land animals.

An array of bird life can also be found in the Keys, from migrating hawks to magnificent frigate birds, and on land, there are the rare Key deer, which roam freely in the lower Keys from No Name and Big Pine Key to the Sugarloaf Keys.

Reef fish at Looe Key coral reef just south of Big Pine Key.

The Key deer is the smallest subspecies of the Virginia white-tailed deer, having become isolated in the middle keys about 4,000 to 10,000 years ago when sea levels rose. They are animals out of a Tolkien novel or indigenous mythology—tiny deer waist high, even full-grown bucks. Many are accustomed to people, although hand feeding is prohibited.

Other rare species include the Schaus' Swallowtail and Miami Blue butterfly and several species of colorful tree snails found only in the Keys.

Besides natural wonders, civilization in the form of great restaurants, lodging, and evening entertainment is found in every Keys town. Thus, the best of both worlds can be experienced. Nevin O. Winter's 1918 description of the Keys still holds true today if you replace the train ride for a vehicle or bicycle ride: "There are many wonderful glimpses of the sea that one obtains on a trip down over the Keys. One realizes this when the train slides off the mainland, down near Everglade, onto the first key, over an extenuated causeway. The Keys at times seem like emeralds in settings of silver floating on seas of lapis lazuli, and the soft trade winds sough through palm and mangrove and bay cedar."

History, too, is a strong part of the Keys experience. Visual reminders of Henry Flagler's overseas railroad of the early 1900s can be seen in the arching concrete columns of several old bridges, including the original Seven Mile Bridge between

Knight's Key and Ohio Key. Remnant railroad depots still exist, and the Flagler Station Over-Sea Railway Historeum can be visited at the Key West Seaport.

At the 5-acre Pigeon Key near Marathon, almost a stone's throw from the modern Seven Mile Bridge, eight century-old buildings are being well maintained for educational and historic purposes, and one houses the Railroad Museum. Several thousand men built the Florida Keys Over-Sea Railroad, and Pigeon Key served as a base camp for those building the original Seven Mile Railroad Bridge. The popular 2.2.-mile span of the old bridge to Pigeon Key has recently been renovated so that pedestrians and bicyclists can continue to access the historic site. A new 60-passenger tram also takes visitors to Pigeon Key.

The most challenging bridge projects for Flagler were the Long Key Viaduct, Knights Key-Moser Channel Bridge (Seven Mile Bridge), Bahia Honda Bridge,

Historic building built by Henry Flagler on Pigeon Key for use by rail workers.

Paddling along the old Seven Mile Bridge that was originally built for the overseas railroad.

and the Key West Terminal. The Seven Mile Bridge alone consisted of 546 concrete foundation piers—more than used for any bridge in the world at the time—210 53-foot arches, 335 80-foot and 60-foot deck plate steel spans, and a 253-foot drawbridge. Each pier built in the main channel for this span required enough sand, gravel, cement, and other materials to fill the cargo hull of a five-masted schooner.

"Never before had such wonderful bridging been attempted," wrote Nevin O. Winter in 1918. "Many said it was absolutely impossible. In one instance, at least, the distance is so great that the horizon closes in on the opposite terminus. In the construction it was necessary to build towers for sighting the instruments, for the curvature of the earth rendered the rodman on the key undistinguishable from the man with transit."

Interestingly, the idea of a railroad to Key West from the mainland was first put forth at the dawn of America's railway era in 1831 by the editor of the *Key West Gazette*. Several plans were hatched through the 1800s, mainly because Key West was Florida's most populous city from around 1840 to 1890. How could the southeast's deepest shipping port—the "American Gibraltar," as one congressman put it—remain isolated from the rest of Florida? When Henry Flagler helped put Miami on the map by extending the Florida East Coast Railway to the city in 1896, the vision of a Keys railroad came into clearer focus. Engineering surveys began in 1902, and the project gained steam when the federal government decided to build the Panama Canal, giving the Key West port even more prominence.

Henry Flagler was 75 years old when he gave his vice president, Joseph Parrott, the green light: "Go ahead. Go to Key West." Perhaps we can understand Flagler's motivation a bit by this 1906 statement: "I have always been contented, but I have never been satisfied." Flagler initially made his fortune by founding the Standard Oil Company with John D. Rockefeller and then funneling his money toward development of the East Coast Railroad and building elaborate hotels along the route. Henry Plant spurred similar growth along Florida's west coast.

A railroad to Key West, once considered Flagler's Folly, was later viewed as a herculean engineering feat and labeled "the eighth wonder of the world." It wasn't economically successful, however, and it suffered a slow decline to bankruptcy. The Labor Day Hurricane of 1935, perhaps the strongest in contemporary Keys history, served as a final blow. But without Flagler showing the way—and leaving sturdy bridge spans from Key Largo to Key West—the Overseas Highway might never have been built. And today, bicyclists and hikers use some of the original railroad spans on the Florida Keys Overseas Heritage Trail, making it one of the most popular state-managed park and trail units in Florida. Kayakers, too, enjoy paddling along the artistic concrete bridge arches built by Flagler, and being on the water, they have a better view of the spans.

German cement was used for most undertakings below the high tide line, a high-quality cement that has been unmatched since it was able to harden in salt water, thus one reason most of the pilings remain solid. To create the pilings, workers built dams around each one to keep out sea water. The total project took years. Thousands of men from a variety of professions, including unskilled laborers from New York's "skid row," were recruited to work. They were housed on various islands and on boats, and dangers from hurricanes and tropical storms were ever present. One boat containing about 150 men broke away from its moorings during a 1906 storm, and 100 men were lost. Less dangerous, but a near constant torment, were the mosquitoes and sand fleas, and this was cited as a primary reason men quit their jobs.

The hurricanes prompted Flagler to focus on sturdier, though more expensive, materials. Concrete arches were preferred in many places over wood and steel trestles since they were more permanent.

The railroad was completed on January 22, 1912. Frail and in poor health at age 83, Flagler rode in on a special train with various distinguished guests. Upon his arrival, he received a grand ovation, and Key West declared a three-day holiday. "Now I can die happy," Flagler told the throngs. "My dream is fulfilled." He died the next year.

Flagler biographer Edward Akin contends that Flagler built the Key West Extension not to enhance his personal wealth or position, but as an enduring monument. "There was no way an aging man would reap a profit from the venture," Akin wrote. "One must view the Key West Extension simply as Henry Flagler's gift to Florida—and his desire to be immortalized." Ironically, Flagler's rail bed and bridges are more successful today in serving a nonmotorized trail than they were when trains chugged to and from Key West. Bicyclists contribute millions each year to the bustling Keys tourism-oriented economy.

Less obvious historic reminders in the Keys are shipwrecks that can sometimes be spotted in the gin-clear waters, testament as to how treacherous the Keys' waters were for navigation. There is even the San Pedro Underwater Archeological Preserve State Park between Upper and Lower Matecumbe Keys where visitors can snorkel or glide over the remains of a 1733 Spanish treasure ship, which lies in 18 feet of water. Five white mooring buoys mark the site.

Salvaging shipwrecks, known as wrecking, was once the main industry in the Keys. The cry of "wreck ashore!" produced massive work stoppages as residents rushed to the unlucky vessel. Salvagers were legally entitled to a portion of the ship's salvaged goods. In today's context, imagine a semi-truck breaking down along the highway and the tow truck operator and his minions legally taking a large share of the cargo. This form of "legal piracy" had closely followed the era of Black Caesar and other noted Keys pirates who ultimately fell to the United States Navy in the early 1800s. Bahamians and Calusa Indians were also known to be early wreckers, and Seminole Indians preyed upon ships and shipwreck survivors during the Second Seminole War, although they spared a stranded French vessel on one occasion stating they were only at war with Americans. Other coastal skirmishes during the war included a deadly night raid on Indian Key led by the "Spanish Indian" Chekika, who was possibly of Calusa descent, and two separate attacks on the Cape Florida Lighthouse.

By the time the United States acquired Florida from Spain, more than 500 seamen using 50 to 60 vessels were employed in the business of wrecking. It usually took several wrecking boats working together to salvage the cargoes of large ships. In many cases, once the heavy cargo was removed, a stranded ship could be freed from a reef and brought to port to be repaired. For ships that sank underwater, wreckers often used divers to help retrieve cargo. Wreckers generally saved the lives of stranded crewmen at no charge, often supplying them with food and safe passage, so in this regard they provided a valuable service.

Besides the wreckers themselves, many others associated with the industry received a percentage of the salvaged goods or its determined value. These included the warehouse merchants, appraisers, and the proctors or lawyers who represented the wreckers and the owners of the property in courts where the breakdown of percentages was determined. In addition, merchants would profit from reselling the merchandise, and carpenters and other workers would often be employed in repairing damaged ships.

The merchants who bought and sold salvaged goods may have profited most from the wrecking industry. The goods, which included precious metals along with satins, laces, and liquors, were often sold at auction in Key West, but because the island was so far away from other cities, only a handful of merchants would be present, and they often worked together to keep prices low. One insurance underwriter complained that a $30,000 cargo might be sold at auction for less than a third of its value. By 1840, Key West became Florida's richest city, and since nearly everyone in the small city benefited from wrecking, it is believed residents had the highest per capita income in the country.

Better mapping of the reefs and the establishment of lighthouses at key locations reduced the amount of shipwrecks along the Keys, thereby cutting into the wrecking business. The changes, especially the lighthouses, prompted one wrecker to lament in 1874, "I wish them x#&! lights was sunk below the sea!"

A 1921 change in the laws regarding wrecking put a final end to a colorful era.

Other bygone Keys industries include turtling—using sea turtles for food, leather, jewelry, and other art forms. The green sea turtle was especially prized for its meat, and its "calipee," the fat attached to the lower shell, became stock for the popular green turtle soup.

The late Florida naturalist Archie Carr, in his classic sea turtle book *So Excellent a Fishe*, expounded on the green turtle's edibility from a historical perspective: "A green turtle was as big as a heifer, easy to catch, and easy to keep alive on its back in a space no greater than itself. It was an ideal food resource, and it went into the cooking pots of the salt-water peasantry and tureens of the flagships alike. It fed a host of people and to some of them it became a dish of almost ceremonial stature. In England the green turtle came to be known as the London Alderman's Turtle, because an Alderman's Banquet was considered grossly incomplete if it failed to begin with clear green turtle soup."

By 1878, 15,000 green turtles a year were being shipped from Florida and the Caribbean to England. Along Florida's coast, turtle meat canning facilities and turtle kraals, where turtles were kept alive in pens until market prices rose to a desired level, were common, especially in Key West.

Sloppy Joe's Bar, once frequented by writer Ernest Hemingway, is a popular Key West landmark.

"At the urging of a New York wholesale grocer, a French chef named Armand Granday opened a cannery on the tropical island at the foot of Margaret Street," wrote Jack Davis in *The Gulf*. "His was the busiest and most famous around. He sold turtle soup in a 1.4-pound can, wrapped in a paper label that claimed the turtles were caught in the 'neighborhood,' though the label's image includes two men turning a green on a beach in front of mountains, despite Key West's being sandpit flat. The caption proclaims, 'Direct from Sea to Kettle.'"

Granday's turtle kraal attracted the attention of tourists, so he began charging a small fee to view the doomed reptiles. Of course, sea turtles started becoming scarce in US waters by the late 1800s, and many had to be imported from the Caribbean and Central America to keep up with demand. It was the Great Plains buffalo slaughter in a marine environment, and the outcome was just as predictable. By the early 1900s, large sea turtles were becoming scarce, and the market collapsed. Eventually, the harvesting of sea turtles and their eggs became illegal as some turtle species approached the brink of extinction.

Today, it is a thrill to see sea turtles in waters of the Keys from a boat or sea kayak, especially knowing they are often on incredible migrational journeys that will take them thousands of miles, navigating by detecting subtle differences in the earth's magnetic field. In fact, seeing the Keys from the water is a great way to experience both tropical splendor and unique culture. The Overseas Highway is busy, and some of the island towns can become congested during the peak winter tourist season—and pricey when it comes to overnight accommodations—but by visiting the many state parks and natural areas and paddling or boating to lush, uninhabited islands or through winding mangrove-canopied tunnels, it is easy to taste wildness and to experience solitude. Conversely, civilization in the form of great restaurants, lodging, and evening entertainment is often within easy reach of the water. Thus, the best of both worlds can be experienced in the Florida Keys.

Miami—the Magic City! It deserves its name. The magic is not only in its waters and its skies, its sunshine and its ocean breezes, but in the spirit which has moved and still moves its people forward and upward to rise above disaster and, filled with pride and determination, carry on towards the goal of making Miami the greatest city of the South."

—FRANK PARKER STOCKBRIDGE AND JOHN HOLLIDAY PERRY,
SO THIS IS FLORIDA, 1938

View of Biscayne Bay
from the Boca Chita
Lighthouse.

MIAMI'S BISCAYNE JEWEL

Creating Miami's Biscayne National Park, the largest marine park in the National Park System, was no easy task. Development in Florida had largely gone unchecked through the 1950s, and it seemed that anyone who had a scheme for a canal, dam, factory, bridge, highway, or large-scale development was successful if they had enough clout and financial backing.

In Biscayne Bay in the 1960s, plans were put forth to dredge up 8,000 acres of bay bottom to build a jetport, a chemical refinery, a new city to be called Islandia, and a major industrial seaport to be known as Seadade. For access, developers hoped to blast a 40-foot-deep channel across the bay and build an overseas highway from Key Biscayne to Key Largo. The green light was about to be flashed when a small but loud band of pesky environmental activists emerged, highlighting the bay's unspoiled islands, clear shallow waters, vast seagrass beds, and outstanding fishing. Their argument: the bay should be protected as a first ever marine national monument.

During the ensuing environmental battle, several attempts were made to intimidate activists, including vandalism, dog poisoning, and pressure on employers. Developers even ran a bulldozer back and forth down the middle of Elliott Key—7 miles long and six lanes wide—in an effort to ruin its potential as a park.

But it pays to have friends in high places, and/or with deep pockets. One of the bay activists to emerge was vacuum cleaner magnate Herbert Hoover Jr. He used his resources to fly lawmakers down to see the bay and garnered the assistance of US representative Dante Fascell of Dade County. Fascell successfully pushed a bill through Congress to create the initial national monument, legislation that President Lyndon B. Johnson would sign into law in 1968 to protect "a rare combination of terrestrial, marine and amphibious life in a tropical setting of great natural beauty." The park's visitor center is named after Fascell.

The park was expanded several times and changed from a national monument to a national park. The current park is now 35 miles long and 8 miles wide—almost 173,000 acres—boasting islands, shallow patch reefs, tropical fish, and even a sunken British warship from 1748. Ninety-five percent of the park is underwater.

And what happened to the six-lane path cut through Elliott Key to spite park activists? It became known as the Spite Highway, and over time, the six-lane path narrowed to one lane, and adjoining trees created a shaded canopy, a testament to nature's recovery powers. Being 7 miles in length, it is the park's only hiking trail of any length.

"The park's founders were a small but committed group who were very persistent. Most didn't have a lot of resources," said park ranger Gary Bremen, who began working at the park in 1989. Park activists and supporters included airline workers from Miami, professors from the University of Miami who saw the bay as a laboratory, a spunky *Miami Herald* environmental reporter named Juanita Greene, and a fishing rod manufacturer, Karl Carman. "I knew most of these people," said Bremen. "Their example is very powerful and emotional to me and I feel moved to carry on what they accomplished. At other national parks like Yosemite, no one

Biscayne National Park ranger Gary Bremen knew most of the park's founders.

Biscayne Bay snorkelers.

can say they knew founders like John Muir, but I knew most of the founders here at Biscayne National Park."

In 2020, the last of the park's founders, former Pan American Airlines employee Lloyd Miller died at the age of 100. "Whenever he came into the visitor center, I made sure everyone stopped what they were doing to meet him," said Bremen. "He was a hero to me, big time." Miller was often called the father of the park.

Bremen and others worry about the park's future. Threats include rising sea levels, leachate from the Turkey Point Nuclear Power Plant and Mount Trashmore (Miami–Dade County's landfill), a change in the volume of freshwater that once flowed into the bay, noise pollution from the Homestead Air Reserve Station, and air pollution caused by the region's heavy road traffic. Then, there is marine debris. "We have found stuff from five continents," said Bremen with a sigh. But the threats have not dampened Bremen's enthusiasm when talking about the bay. "This is my favorite place in the whole world," he said.

Unfolding a park map, Bremen pointed out some of his favorite areas, including the remote and scenic Jones Lagoon where he got married in 2018 to his long-time sweetheart. The Lagoon was named after the Jones family, who purchased nearby Porgy Key in 1897. The African American family raised and sold pineapples and limes. Eventually, only one member of the family remained on the island, Sir Lancelot Jones, Lance for short. He became famous as a fishing guide, having the distinction of taking several US presidents fishing. Later, Jones acknowledged that Herbert Hoover was the best angler of the lot while Warren Harding was the worst.

Known fondly as "the philosopher of Porgy Key" and "the soul of Biscayne Bay," Jones once described his life on Porgy Key: "I am alone but I'm not lonely. When you have plenty of interests like the water and woods, the birds and the fish, you don't get lonely."

When developers in the 1960s wanted to buy his 277-acre island and smaller islands he owned for their grand schemes, he refused to sell, holding up their plans. Eventually, he and his sister-in-law sold their holdings to the federal government for the national park, as long as Lance could remain for as long as he wished. Jones would often visit nearby Adams Key Environmental Education Center and share with visitors his knowledge of marine life, especially regarding native sponges that he continued to harvest and sell. "One of my most prized possessions is a Lance-harvested glove sponge, purchased at Adams Key when he was selling sponges to school kids when it was still permitted in the park," said Gary Bremen.

When Hurricane Andrew bore down in 1992, park rangers persuaded the then 94-year-old Jones to leave the island. The next day, the storm obliterated his island home, and Jones lived his remaining five years on the mainland. Today, visitors can view concrete foundations of his house and that of his family and imagine their island existence.

Because it is a marine park, the primary way to access Biscayne National Park is by boat or sea kayak. The Biscayne National Park Institute, a nonprofit organization that pumps extra revenues back into the park, rents kayaks and takes visitors on boating and snorkeling trips, working out of the park's visitor center near Homestead. One can also use a number of private tour companies along with personal watercraft to experience the park.

Guests on a tour boat watch dolphins feed in Biscayne Bay.

The Boca Chita Lighthouse, built by a previous landowner and not authorized for actual use, is a popular stop for boat tours in Biscayne Bay. The island was once a playground for the rich and famous and is now part of Biscayne National Park.

Boating across the bay on a calm day, with the water clear and teeming with sea turtles, sharks, stingrays and schools of bottlenose dolphins and other marine life, it is easy to fall under a spell of adventure and wonder. One gazes into the shallow bay waters and scans the lush uninhabited islands, and because the park is so large, it never feels crowded, even though around 500,000 people visit annually.

One reason the establishment of Biscayne National Park was successful is due to the intense development of adjoining mainland areas and islands; some old-timers remembered the quaint village of "Miam-uh" of the early 1900s. When Miami was incorporated in 1896, the year Henry Flagler reached the town with his East Coast Railroad, it boasted 1,681 residents. Some settlers were content with keeping Miami a tropical paradise for themselves, having purchased vast tracts for paltry sums, but Julia Tuttle had a different vision. A mover and shaker who moved to the town permanently in 1891 after her husband's death, she dreamed of Miami's future. "All these years I have had but one thought, and that thought is to see

Miami grow to be one of the largest if not the largest, city in all the southland," she told Flagler lieutenant F. E. Ingraham. She even proposed to name the town after Flagler, an honor he refused, but Flagler did open a key land corridor to Miami partly because the town's orange crop was unscathed after the hard freeze of 1895, making the area more attractive to winter visitors and investors. What other town in the Eastern United States could escape winter's harshest grasp?

Miami grew steadily over the next few years, claiming 5,471 residents a decade after its founding, but the boom would not come until another mover and shaker came on the scene, Carl Fisher. Starting in 1912, Fisher and other investors took a biologically rich mangrove swamp with an oceanside sand beach and turned it into one of the swankiest coastal resorts the world has ever seen—Miami Beach. The former mangrove swamp became the anchor for what is now known as the Gold Coast. Fisher also purchased several smaller islands in Biscayne Bay so he could bring influential people to fish and party.

At first, in developing Miami Beach, Fisher hired crews to hand clear the mangroves and palmettos, and Fisher even jumped in himself. His wife Jane wrote: "The palmettos were almost impossible even for mules to uproot with chains and grappling hooks. I have seen Carl tugging with his hands at a small palmetto, trying to break it free from the sand, cursing until I stopped my ears.

"The mangroves, with their canopy of glistening green leaves, were fascinating; but steely roots showered from the tips to fasten the trees to the ground with a network strong as metal mesh. The vice-like roots defied the heaviest axes."

Only when Fisher brought in heavy equipment did he successfully clear the mangrove and palmetto jungles on Miami Beach and fill in the soggy bottom with sand, mud, and marl dredged from Biscayne Bay. The state and federal governments granted Fisher free permits to dredge millions of cubic yards of bay bottom in a project never before attempted on such a scale. The land rose to 5 feet above the high tide line. It was the type of large-scale coastal development that would be emulated in other parts of Florida. Need land? Just dredge it up from the bay bottoms. And why not cut mazes of finger canals so every lot was "waterfront property" and every homeowner had direct boat access to prime fishing waters?

Roads were next for Fisher because, by this time, America was becoming enamored with the automobile. Fisher helped build a long bridge to his paradise, and streets were put in on his island as soon as the fill dried.

Fisher and his partners soon realized that landscaping had to follow due to ensuing sandstorms. Mulch was brought in from the Everglades to create the proper soil. Hundreds of laborers then planted grass, shrubs, and trees, including bougainvillea, hibiscus, oleander, poinciana, and orchid trees. A "tropical paradise" was being born. By 1915, Fisher was constructing a golf course, tennis courts, and a 300-foot pier, and he was planning a hotel, office buildings, and his own elaborate home. Almost 200 house lots were sold, and a sewer line led straight into the bay. Still, the wildness of the place was not completely quelled. Mosquitoes could be ferocious; snakes still inhabited the island, and American crocodiles sunned along the beach as they had for millennia.

To complete his vision, Fisher realized northerners would need to come to Miami in larger numbers than those who were arriving by train and by boat. A highway was needed, a long highway from northern cities to Miami, and so the idea of the Dixie Highway was born. Eventually, more than one route was established, but they all converged at Miami Beach. To help advertise his growing empire, Fisher acquired a baby elephant named Rosie to romp along his beach and serve as President Warren G. Harding's golf caddy—a fun photo op—but his wife Jane would inadvertently begin the largest advertising draw. As described in my book *Nostalgic Florida*, Jane disliked the cumbersome bathing attire for women of the time. So, she shortened material here and there to make swimming more comfortable. Other young women followed her lead. Carl Fisher seized on the new trend.

"We'll get the prettiest girls we can find and put them in the goddamned tightest and shortest bathing suits and no stockings or swim shoes either," he said. "We'll have their pictures taken and send them all over the goddamn country as 'The Bathing Beauties of Miami Beach'!" A slogan for the photos was developed: "It's always June in Miami Beach."

Florida's iconic "bathing beauty" imagery was born.

When the Florida land boom heated up in 1925, Miami Beach was front and center, and Fisher reaped the rewards. The trains and roads leading to Florida became clogged with hopeful investors, and the congestion persisted long after the winter "snowbird" season ended. Agents hawked real estate on Miami streets, and books, magazines, and newspapers assured investors that the boom would last and their investments would grow. "Florida is America's last great frontier," wrote Charles Donald Fox in the 1925 book *The Truth about Florida*. "Its conquest invites the sons and daughters of those whose accomplishments in sister states have made the nation what it is. . . . [T]hose who come at this time will be looked upon ten years hence as pioneers."

Fox assured his would-be pioneer readers that "the so-called 'boom' will last forever, for there can be no let-up to the development of a state which offers so much to so many classes of people." He added that the boom was "turning the tables on the usual development procedure—it is speeding up the future and making it the present."

Everything spoke of unending bounty and profit making, including an article by Hullin Spencer in *Suniland Magazine* titled "Spinners of Gold in Florida." "The boom that is sweeping Florida is like the golden web hovering over the land. It is as if a great unseen spinner sat at his weaving attaching his thread to one point after another in the State filling it with the glow of promise and achievement, and from these vantage points spinning broader, wider, embracing more and more territory, drawing more and more people into its friendly meshes, and holding them voluntary prisoners because of the splendid lure of opportunity."

The Cape Florida Lighthouse, first erected in 1825, preceded the building booms in the Miami area. It survived hurricanes and even an attack by Seminole Indians in 1836.

Stiltsville, houses built on stilts in Biscayne Bay, dates back to the 1930s. Only a few structures remain, and they are now part of Biscayne National Park.

The infamous 1925 land boom bottomed out the next year, and a devastating Miami hurricane gave its demise an exclamation point. In 1929, the stock market crashed, and America sunk into the depths of the Great Depression. Carl Fisher's financial fortunes crashed as well, but Miami Beach and the rest of Miami lived on to thrive again.

Today, the Miami area is a cosmopolitan place with a Latin beat, eclectic and worldly, with a pulsing night life. From Biscayne Bay at night, the panorama of Miami's lighted skyline is among the most dramatic anywhere. From a quaint town just over a century ago, Miami's metro area is now home to more than six million souls. Julia Tuttle, the only woman to have founded a large American city, would be proud. But Biscayne Bay also gleams just offshore—the first national marine park of its kind—and there are several mainland state parks that allow for wonderful natural retreats, including Bill Baggs Cape Florida and Oleta River state parks.

Florida has long been a state of dreamers, where individuals sought to transform the land and waters to their will, whether it be large-scale developments, railroads, or theme parks, but it is also known for its stubborn conservationists who sought to protect unique places and allow for them to exist as they always have. Biscayne Bay is such a place.

Facing page: A palm-lined walkway to the Cape Florida Lighthouse in Bill Baggs Cape Florida State Park.

The sun disappeared and the wind increased in velocity coming from the east and east northeast. The seas became very giant in size, the wind continued blowing us toward shore, pushing us into shallow water. It soon happened that we were unable to use any sail at all . . . and we were at the mercy of the wind and water, always driven closer to shore. Having then lost all of our masts, all of the ships were wrecked on the shore, and with the exception of mine, broke to pieces.

—MIGUEL DE LIMA, OWNER OF THE SPANISH SHIP *URCA DE LIMA*,
WHICH SUNK NEAR PRESENT-DAY FORT PIERCE IN 1715

Gold coins displayed at the Museum of Florida History in Tallahassee as part of a 1715 Plate Fleet shipwreck exhibit.

OF SHIPWRECKS AND SPANISH TREASURE

Florida's reefs were never kind to early sailing ships. Wreckages literally line Florida's east coast, especially southeast Florida because the Gulf Stream lies closer to land than in any other part of North America.

The most famous shipwreck was a Spanish fleet laden with gold and silver from Mexico and Peru in the vicinity of Sebastian Inlet in 1715. It was called the Plate Fleet since it carried large quantities of silver, *plata* being the Spanish word for silver.

The flotilla numbered 12 ships, and they left Havana with great fanfare on July 24, 1715, with flags flying, crowds cheering, anchors being hoisted, and sails unfurling. Soon, the great fleet, bedecked with colorful banana and plantain stalks and hampers of fresh coconuts, oranges and limes, began moving out of the harbor. Below deck, the ships were loaded down with cargo and 14 million pesos worth of the king's treasure along with chests of private wealth.

As the ships moved out of the harbor, their passengers waved last farewells, and drums rolled from Morro Castle high above the water. A black-robed archbishop blessed the fleet. Then, the castle's cannons roared 12 times, and the ships answered in kind. Spain had become increasingly dependent upon gold and silver from the New World to meet its needs, and so the safe passage of each treasure fleet was vitally important for the ambitious country. With good fortune, the fleet would reach Seville within two months.

The first part of their journey was uneventful with favorable winds and seas, but as the fleet neared Florida, ominous clouds in the south and southeast were seen. Swells slowly increased, and the midday sky took on a milky haze. Some mariners used clear vials of shark oil as a weather forecaster. They would turn cloudy with the approach of a bad storm, and surely the vials must have turned cloudy on this day. Also, seasoned sailors likely complained of sore joints, another indicator of foul weather.

Soon, stinging squalls struck the fleet, the ships rocking violently from side to side, threatening to send sailors into churning waters. All who were aboard were frightened, miserable, and praying for their lives. Giant waves began crashing over decks. Sails shredded, and masts broke and shattered. Crews frantically tried to untangle rigging and lighten loads to avoid the shoals they knew were nearby, but one by one, ships were smashed onto the southeast Florida reefs by the hurricane's fury. Eleven ships, 14 million pesos, and 700 people were claimed by the sea. Only one ship, a captured French frigate, escaped the storm's wrath because it had sailed far ahead of the fleet, its crew not even aware that a hurricane was nearby.

For a 30-mile stretch of beach, from present-day Cape Canaveral to Fort Pierce, bodies and wreckage were strewn across the water line. The 1,500 survivors, some badly injured, ended up in several different groups. Fires were built, bodies were buried, boxes and barrels were dragged above the tide line, and people worried about hostile Ais Indians. But it was some of the lower-class passengers and seamen who posed the biggest threat. Looting of bodies and unclaimed personal belongings became commonplace, there being few authoritative figures with useable weapons to enforce order.

Eventually, the survivor camps merged closer together for safety reasons. Crude shelters were built, and people began to fish, harvest shellfish and other marine life, and snare animals. Since it was summer, biting bugs plagued the group, and those normally accustomed to an upper-crust existence were nearly driven mad. Some died from exposure to the elements. Fortunately for the group, three large launch boats were salvaged from the ships. Two were to be outfitted with mostly women, children, and the injured and sail to St. Augustine, about 120 miles to the north, but some of the looters tried to bribe their way onto the boats. Rebuffed, they set out for St. Augustine on foot with their newfound wealth.

The commander of the survivors, Admiral Salmon, sent two letters to the Spanish governor in St. Augustine with the boats. One letter discreetly addressed the looter group: "I wish to communicate to you, in confidence, after having sent to you another letter with the pilot, that my men have revolted and are leaving this camp for your garrison heavily loaded with the silver they have stolen. Please, have them arrested and deprived of what they have unlawfully taken." The largest launch boat sailed back toward Havana in hopes that a salvage party could be organized and the treasure recovered. Many individuals of high rank and wealth were on board, thereby escaping the hardships of the castaway camps.

When the first longboat and Admiral Salmon's dispatches reached Governor Orioles in St. Augustine, the governor immediately prohibited any person from leaving the city without a permit and ordered all boats to be guarded to prevent unauthorized individuals from going after the king's treasure. He also ordered the shipwrecked looters, who would soon arrive on foot, to be intercepted and stripped of their ill-gotten gains. And even though drought had limited food production around St. Augustine, supplies were quickly sent to shipwreck survivors at the beach camps. Ais Indians also began to help, to the surprise of many, constructing thatched huts and teaching survivors how to eat cabbage palms, sea grapes, and palmetto berries, and to sun dry and smoke meat.

Seven ships sailed from Havana to rescue the castaways and especially, the treasure. Included in the group were 30 free divers, some of whom were coastal Indian pearl divers from South America. By mid-September, the shipwreck survivors were returned to Havana, but the long and dangerous treasure salvaging had only begun. Divers dove down with ropes in churning, murky water to tie around treasure chests to be hoisted up. Several perished in the process, but within a few months, most of the king's treasure was recovered and brought to shore. Still, all was not safe. Word of the lost treasure fleet had spread on the high seas, and the lure of lightly guarded gold and silver was irresistible as it had been for millennia. Some salvage ships were intercepted by pirates on their return to Havana. And much of the private wealth from the treasure ships—thousands of silver and gold coins— still lay on the ocean's bottom, to be found bit by bit by 20th-century beachgoers and in larger troves by more sophisticated treasure hunters. The McLarty Treasure Museum in Sebastian Inlet State Park recounts the story.

No wonder this part of Florida's shore has become known as the Treasure Coast.

Another notable Treasure Coast shipwreck occurred in 1696 when Quaker merchant Jonathan Dickinson became shipwrecked along the coast near Peck Lake, a few miles above present-day Jupiter. Shipwrecks are bad enough, but for Dickinson and his men, their ordeal was only the beginning. "The wilderness country looked very dismal, having no trees," Dickinson later wrote, "but only sand hills covered with shrubby palmetto, the stalks of which were prickly, that there was no walking amongst them."

In trying to walk to St. Augustine along the beach, Dickinson and his crew were captured by Jobe or Hobe (Hoe-Bay) Indians and marched south to their main village along Jupiter Inlet, site of the present-day DuBois Park and Jupiter Inlet Lighthouse & Museum. "After we had traveled about five miles along the deep sand, the sun being extremely hot, we came to an inlet," Dickinson wrote. "On the other side was the Indian town, being little wigwams made of small poles stuck in the ground, which they bended one to another, making an arch, and covered them with thatch of small palmetto-leaves." The shipwreck survivors learned to bury themselves in sand to avoid the mosquito hordes while the Indians often used bear grease and fish oil. Eventually, they were released, whereupon they walked north several days to St. Augustine.

The Gilbert's Bar House of Refuge was built on Hutchison Island in 1876 to rescue shipwreck survivors along Florida's southeast coast.

Bedroom for shipwreck survivors in the Gilbert's Bar House of Refuge.

Large lifeboat used for rescues at Gilbert's Bar House of Refuge.

Over time, Indian tribes along the southeast coast were largely vanquished due to disease and war, but white settlement was sparse throughout the 1700s and 1800s. Shipwrecks continued, however, and survivors who made it to shore had to struggle to survive. If medical attention was needed, a doctor was often more than 100 miles away. The US Life-Saving Service, predecessor to the US Coast Guard, responded by building 10 "houses of refuge" along the east coast with the mission of rescuing shipwreck survivors. The last of those houses, the Gilbert's Bar House of Refuge on Hutchison Island, is now a museum and Martin County's oldest building.

Constructed in 1876 on the "St. Lucie Rocks," the Gilbert's Bar House of Refuge fulfilled its purpose several times during its early days. In October 1904, for example, shipwrecks occurred on two consecutive days within sight of the house.

As Florida became more developed, and the US Coast Guard became more sophisticated in responding to emergencies at sea, the need for houses of refuge dwindled. Most were abandoned, succumbing to storms and hurricanes. Fortunately, the Gilbert's Bar House of Refuge survives because it was used during World War II as a lookout station to spot German U-boats, and it was later purchased by Martin County for a museum. The house resembles an early bed and breakfast with several rooms and beds and a large kitchen. The commanding view from the front porch makes one realize why the spot was chosen.

Seminole Indians salvaged some shipwrecks, such as one near Pompano Beach in 1858, and early American pioneers of the southeast Florida coast combed the beaches for lumber and other useful items washed up from shipwrecks, especially after several ships went down in the hurricane of August 1870. "Quantities of copper and brass in bolts, nails, and sheet form were found that could be traded in at the store at Sand Point [Titusville] for anything in stock; the store owner gave ten cents a pound for brass and fifteen for copper," wrote Charles W. Pierce in *Pioneer Life in Southeast Florida*. "I obtained my first school slate in trade for a copper bolt found on the beach. This junk metal was the bank on which the first settlers drew for their food, clothes, and ammunition for their guns."

During one period in 1877, Pierce noted that a new settler located the site of his homestead on a beach ridge but that "exceptionally good weather had prevailed in the Gulf Stream during the past six months and no vessels had lost their loads of lumber, so Dexter was compelled to defer his building operations while waiting for stormy weather." Why purchase lumber when it would eventually just wash up for free?

Shipwrecks also provided surprises. In 1878, the Spanish ship *Providencia* washed up in the Lake Worth area with a huge load of coconuts. Nearby settlers descended upon the wreck, and within a short period, planted hundreds of the coconuts all over their homesteads. As a result, this stretch of coast would eventually be known as "Palm Beach."

Another welcome surprise occurred in 1886 when hundreds of casks of Spanish wine washed up on the beach from Indian River to Biscayne Bay in what became known as "the Great Wine Wreck." On one stretch of beach, Pierce reported that the wine casks were "so close together one could have walked for a mile along this part of the beach without once having to step off a cask." The party lasted for weeks.

The beaches also provided food in the form of loggerhead, green, hawksbill, and leatherback sea turtles along with their eggs laid in May, June, and part of July. According to Pierce, the turtle eggs were "boiled, scrambled, put into pancakes, cake, and egg bread, but they were never fried since the white of a turtle egg will not cook hard." Pierce added that Florida black bears also sought the eggs, so during turtle nesting season, pioneers successfully hunted for bear along the beach.

Mosquitoes and sand flies were the enemy of early pioneers, and for a long time, Pierce's family home did not have bug screens. "Light would attract the mosquitoes, so we spent our evenings after supper sitting in the dark and talking of friends and neighbors we had left in Waukegan, Illinois," he wrote. "In the middle of the room a smoke pot poured forth volumes of rank fumes that at least kept out a portion of the hungry mosquitoes that were so eager to get at us to satisfy their bloody appetites."

For early settlers, mail service was a luxury, and there was no mail service between the Lake Worth Country around Hypoluxo to Miami. After a failed two-year attempt, the United States Postal Service began employing carriers in 1884 to walk an 80-mile route along the beach while carrying a large haversack and adding another 56 miles by boat. The carriers would become known as the Barefoot Mailmen. Once in Miami, the carrier would get some rest and return the same way. Back at Hypoluxo, they would rest one day and do it all over again, all for $600 a year.

One carrier, James "Ed" Hamilton, reached Hillsboro Inlet on the way to Miami in 1887. The small boat that was supposed to be hidden had been taken to the other side by another traveler, so Hamilton waded into the water to swim the inlet. He was never heard from again, his fate unknown. The building of a through road in 1893 followed by Henry Flagler's East Coast Railroad ended the colorful era of the barefoot mailmen.

Much has changed in this part of Florida since Pierce's day. Human population growth and development has skyrocketed. But thanks to the efforts of state and local officials and private citizens, several premier parks provide a glimpse into early coastal Florida. And after large storms, beachcombers still occasionally find gold and silver coins from early Spanish shipwrecks.

For the same reason shipping was close to shore in this stretch of coast because of the Gulf Stream, sportfishing remains an ever-popular sport. "Giant denizens of the sea can be captured in the blue waters of the Gulf Stream," wrote Charles Donald Fox in the 1925 book *The Truth about Florida*. "Experienced guides, bronzed by years of angling in these waters, await the chartering of their swift, practical little sailing vessels, and so handy are the fishing grounds that often a half day suffices to fill the fish box and send the happy fishermen home with their trophies." The Sebastian Fishing Museum in Melbourne Beach chronicles this region's famous fishing history.

In regard to sea turtles, their numbers have rebounded since the days of wanton exploitation. The Treasure Coast generally ranks the highest for loggerhead and leatherback sea turtle nesting in Florida, while Brevard County to the north often has the highest green sea turtle nests.

All five species of Florida sea turtles are either threatened or endangered under the Endangered Species Act, and three regularly nest on Florida beaches—the loggerhead, green, and leatherback. In fact, Florida hosts about 90 percent of all loggerhead nests in the world, and nesting of the green sea turtle has gone up exponentially. The Kemp's ridley and hawksbill nest in very small numbers in Florida with the Kemp's ridley being the most endangered in the world. In any given year, sea turtles make between 40,000 and 84,000 nests along Florida shores, mostly from May to October, although some leatherbacks start as early as February. After about a two-month incubation period, the hatchlings make their way to the sea at night in a precarious struggle for survival. Crabs, raccoons, birds, fish, and other animals prey on the hatchlings, and only about one in 1,000 survive to adulthood. Human predation of sea turtles includes illegal harvesting of turtle eggs, destruction of beach nesting areas, and turtles being hooked or caught in nets. Historically, turtles have also been killed for meat, shells, leather, perfumes, and cosmetics, practices that continue in some countries.

Close-up of a rescued loggerhead sea turtle recovering from sickness in an aquarium.

For Native Americans, sea turtles and their eggs were an important source of food, but sea turtles were also part of a creation myth for some tribes. When the earth was covered with water, turtle dove to the ocean floor to build up earth, and in some stories, the earth was piled onto a turtle's back, creating land. For this reason, the Iroquois people refer to the Earth as Turtle Island, and at some Muscogee ceremonial grounds, the sea turtle is honored with a special dance that creates the shape of a giant turtle on the cleared, sandy earth. Sand is periodically spread on the ceremonial grounds to symbolize first land, and a ring of oyster shells around the grounds marks its boundary.

Some natural features along the Treasure Coast have changed little over millennia. One is the Savannahs Preserve State Park near Port St. Lucie, which protects the largest remnant of freshwater coastal marsh on Florida's east coast. The 10-mile strip of wet prairie can easily be explored by kayak or canoe unless during a dry period, and there are 17 miles of multiuse land trails in the park that are enjoyed by hikers, bicyclists, and horseback riders. Sandhill cranes are commonly seen.

Most of this type of wet prairie environment was initially dredged and drained for winter vegetable crops since Fort Pierce was known as the "Pineapple Capital of the World" from 1895 to 1920. Developers building towns and subdivisions continued the wetlands destruction. As author Bob Rountree noted, "The stunning reality is that to get there, you drive through miles of suburban sprawl from Jensen Beach to Fort Pierce."

Sculpted rocks at Blowing Rocks Preserve near Jupiter.

Another coastal natural area is the largest stretch of rocky Anastasia limestone shoreline along the Atlantic coast along Jupiter Island. Now known as the Blowing Rocks Preserve, managed by the Nature Conservancy, extreme high tides and storms can force plumes of water 50 feet skyward when waves crash onto the rocks. It is a scene more reminiscent of Hawaii than Florida. Blowing Rocks is just one of many surprises one can find along southeast Florida's Treasure Coast.

The Jupiter Lighthouse, bedecked with holiday cheer in December, beams into the night.

FROM ROCKETS TO KAYAKS

While Florida has had boom and bust growth cycles for generations, mostly centered on too-good-to-be-true land (or swamp) deals, Titusville's economy largely revolved around the ups and downs of the space industry ever since the first rocket was launched from Cape Canaveral in 1950. Why the Florida coast? The adjacent open water provided a safe place for booster rockets and fuel tanks to fall. Plus, Florida is closer to the equator than any other state, and a rocket launched near the equator requires less fuel to reach orbit.

From an area that relied mostly on fishing, farming, and ranching, the space industry created highly skilled and good paying jobs in and around Titusville. The Brevard County population zoomed from 23,653 in 1950 to more than 111,000 a decade later. The huge influx of people caused a housing shortage along with crowded roads and schools, and some new workers slept in their vehicles or commuted long distances. As a result, a new residential community was established in 1957, Satellite Beach. The town's oldest building, an Episcopal church built in 1902, was floated in by barge from Fort Pierce in 1959.

When high-profile launches were set to take place, such as John Glenn's 1962 takeoff to become the first American to orbit earth, space tourists swarmed to the area for a vicarious rocket launch experience. The ground rumbled and smoke billowed while the projectile was launched into a gravity-free environment.

Monthly Street party in downtown Titusville with roads closed off to vehicles.

Metaphorically, you could say that Titusville, with its growing system of trails, is where America is heading. The demand and use of trails point to an inspiring rise in values that we all increasingly share health and fitness, clean air, lessening roadway congestion, adding safety to how we otherwise move around, and improving household economy.

—HERB HILLER, *FLORIDA TODAY*, 2016

Local businesses such as motels and restaurants boomed. Florida's Space Coast was born. Other high-profile launches included the *Apollo 11* launch to the moon in 1969, and the first space shuttle launch in 1981.

But when each new space program was discontinued, thousands of workers were laid off and the local economy slumped, such as when the Apollo program dissolved in 1975. It would often take years for a new program to gear up. When the last space shuttle landed in 2011, Titusville braced for another economic blow. Town leaders decided it was time to diversify its economy. They gauged the area's resources and attributes and decided to focus on ecotourism. The town began promoting fishing and birdwatching, hosting an international birding festival every year, and entrepreneurs also began promoting kayaking in the adjacent Merritt Island National Wildlife Refuge, especially on summer nights to witness glowing bioluminescence in the water caused by harmless organisms called dinoflagellates.

Besides watersports, it also became apparent to town leaders that Titusville sat at the crossroads of three long-distance paved bicycle trails being developed—the 250-mile Florida Coast-to-Coast Trail from St. Petersburg to Titusville, the Maine to Florida East Coast Greenway, and the 260-mile St. Johns River-to-Sea Loop. With lengths ranging from 250 miles to 3,000 miles, all three trails promised to draw bicycle tourists from around the world.

In 2013, the town began taking earnest steps to provide amenities and safe passage for bicyclists by forming a trails committee. Once a plan was developed, they built a bicycle/pedestrian bridge over their busiest thoroughfare, Garden Street, revamped downtown streets to be more bicycle and pedestrian friendly, and

Titusville's welcome center with a bike shop inside provides a clear message to visitors that the town is bike friendly.

Indian River Lagoon at the Haulover Canal.

opened a new visitor center in 2017 that included a bike shop inside! The center began averaging 1,000 visitors a month from all parts of the United States and from several countries.

To fine-tune their efforts, town planners also took a field trip to Dunedin, long recognized as being bicycle and pedestrian friendly and crowned Florida's first trail town in 2018. As a result of their efforts, Titusville was designated Florida's second official trail town by the Florida Greenways and Trails Council a few months later. The town's new moniker became "Gateway to Nature and Space."

"The city recognizes the economic impact and importance of becoming a Trail Town," said then mayor Walt Johnson. "We continue to work diligently to become the premier destination and Trail Town in the state. Our downtown merchants are excited and beginning to see the increase in their businesses by those trail users who eat, shop, and enjoy our unique offerings."

Today, area visitors have a choice of riding a bicycle on paved off-highway trails in several directions, including toward the coast. The Merritt Island National Wildlife Refuge is a huge draw with its many mangrove islands in the Indian River Lagoon that attract scores of wading birds. Some are off limits to humans since they serve as bird rookeries. The 156-mile-long Indian River Lagoon is known for having the highest variety of wildlife than any North American estuary, boasting 370 bird species, 685 types of fish, and 29 mammal species. Fifty-three of these species have been deemed threatened or endangered.

Manatees often abound in these waters, although numbers have diminished due to a die-off of native sea grasses from water pollution and associated algae blooms. In 2021, state wildlife officials approved an unprecedented trial plan of feeding manatees romaine lettuce in an effort to stave off starvation in the Indian River Lagoon.

Just to the north, the Canaveral National Seashore provides a development-free beach experience of coastal beauty. This section of coast marks the beginning of the Surf Coast due to its high-energy wave action and popularity with surfers. The Surf Coast's indisputable capital is Daytona Beach farther north, also a mecca for motor-cyclists, NASCAR lovers, and spring breakers. It is one of the few places along Florida's coast where one can still drive a vehicle on the hard-packed beach sand at low tide, carrying on a tradition that began when cars were first introduced on the American scene and early speed trials were held between Daytona Beach and Ormond Beach. Fifteen land speed records were set on the beach between 1905 and 1935 before speed trials were moved to the wider Bonneville Salt Flats in Utah.

At the Canaveral National Seashore, a slower pace is encouraged, especially if exploring a unique place with a scary name, the Mosquito Lagoon. A maze of waterways encircle islands of various sizes, many of which are open for primitive camping with a permit. Mosquitoes can harass visitors in the warmer months, but cooler months make for a kayak and canoe camping paradise. And not to be missed is the massive Native American shell midden, Turtle Mound—50 feet tall and once used by sailors as a navigational marker since it was visible several miles out to sea. And nearby is the Eldora historic settlement, a steamboat stop in the late 1800s.

Beach entrance for vehicles at Daytona Beach

A remote beach at the Canaveral National Seashore.

Visitors also have a choice of several pristine beaches, this being the longest stretch of undeveloped Atlantic coastline in Florida.

Two of Cape Canaveral's beaches are known for being "clothing optional"—Apollo Beach and the Volusia County side of Playalinda Beach since public nudity is prohibited in Brevard County. They are featured in a Visit Florida article on the subject since there are several recognized clothing optional beaches in the state. Nudists help drive Florida's tourist economy, too! It seems that any remote and beautiful beach is clothing optional, although some are more urban, such as Haulover Beach between Miami and Fort Lauderdale.

When I was in my early 20s and doing a lot of backpacking, I sought a coastal wilderness experience and found the remotest beach I could find—Cape San Blas in St. Joseph Peninsula State Park. The rugged peninsula extends more than 8 miles from the beach parking area. I obtained a primitive camping permit and began backpacking where water met sand, dodging in and out of surf like a small shorebird. Most of the beachgoers were near the parking area, so after about 3 miles of walking, there was only sea oats, tall dunes, and the mantra of rolling water. Coastal wilderness! Suddenly, from behind a dune 50 yards ahead, a young naked couple burst out and began playing in the surf, splashing and laughing. I'm sure they thought they were Adam and Eve all alone in a new world. As I came closer, the woman turned and screeched, "Doug!?" It was a friend of mine with her boyfriend out for a frolic, and I'm sure they didn't expect to see anyone, much less me. It was the first and only time I saw her in the buff.

An old homestead at Seminole Rest sits atop an ancient shell mound.

On the mainland side of the Mosquito Lagoon in Oak Hill, Seminole Rest is another must-see stop managed by the National Park Service, but clothing should be worn or arrest may result. This is the site of a group of Timucuan shell middens, the tallest being 18 feet, as well an early residence and caretaker's house from the late 1800s. Shell middens were refuse piles from early Native Americans in coastal regions who ate large amounts of shellfish, such as oysters and clams. A striking complement to the mounds at Seminole Rest are ancient cedars and live oaks that have been twisted by storms and age, bonsai-like in their appearance.

During a time when shell mounds in the area were being bulldozed, the shells being used to build roads and railroad beds, the Snyder family at Seminole Rest refused to sell the mounds on their property for fear it would ruin the ambiance of the place along with the protective elevation the mounds provided. They named their place after Seminole Indians, even though they were helping to preserve a visible vestige of the Timucuan people who thrived along the lagoon between 2000 BCE and 1565 CE, an estimated span of 175 generations! One can imagine the reprimands of Timucuan parents to their children regarding the daily disposal of refuse: "Take the shells and broken pottery to the top of the mound. Not to the side, not by our front door, but to the top!"

A nearby mound called Oak Hill Mound or Sam's Mound did not fare so well. It was bulldozed in 1918 for road fill, the shells reportedly filling 2,000 railroad cars. "When they were taking down Sam's Mound, I went down there often after I got out of school and I had quite a collection of pottery and stuff like that," said former resident Jacqueline Snyder Stevens. Fortunately, a few area mounds were protected and can be appreciated today.

If exploring this section of coast, take note that people have been motoring along US 1, part of which was the original Dixie Highway of the 1920s, for several generations. Some of the oldest motels, usually motor courts laid out in a crescent moon design, bear exotic names such as Shangri-la, Tuscan, and Paradise, keying on early Florida promotional themes.

To the south of Titusville, Old Florida can be experienced in historic Cocoa Village, the Eau Gallie Arts District, and Honest Johns Fish Camp. The fish camp was begun as a government homestead in 1887 in South Melbourne Beach. A two-story 1899 heart pine house still occupies the camp, sitting on its original coquina pilings. The business rents boats and kayaks and sells fishing supplies.

Near Sebastian, another bit of history can be explored, and this one is for the birds. A tiny mangrove-covered island sits among many in the midst of the Indian River Lagoon—Pelican Island. Why is Pelican Island significant? This is where the greatest wildlife refuge system in the world was born in 1903. President Theodore Roosevelt, an avid hunter and bird lover, heeded the cries of ornithologist Frank Chapman and other conservationists by protecting the last known brown pelican

A brown pelican sits on a signpost at Pelican Island, the country's first national wildlife refuge.

rookery on the East Coast. Plume hunters had devastated the rest. A line was drawn in the sand to stem the tide of wanton wildlife destruction before it was too late for the brown pelican and many other species.

Today, Pelican Island has admittedly lost a bit of its former grandeur. From 5.5 acres and 5,000 pelican pairs in the early days, the island has eroded down to 2.2 acres and less than 100 pelican pairs. Fortunately, brown pelicans have repopulated old haunts along with newer spoil islands in establishing several other rookeries. Part of their success is because Pelican Island was protected and used as a launch pad for expanding bird populations.

While boaters and paddlers must stay a safe distance from the island's nesting pelicans, Frank Chapman set up a blind on the island in 1905 and wrote down his observations for *Century Magazine*: "Birds of all ages and voices, from the grunting, naked, squirming new-born chick, or the screaming, downy youngster, to the silent, dignified, white-headed parent, were now within a radius of a few yards. At a glance, I could see most of the activities of pelican home life: nest building, laying, incubating, feeding and brooding young, bathing, preening, sleeping, fighting—all could be observed at arm's length. Surely here was a rare opportunity to add a footnote to our knowledge of animal life."

From its humble beginning, more than 560 national wildlife refuges, representing almost 100 million acres, have been established. Refuges are now found in all 50 states as well as American Samoa, Puerto Rico, Virgin Islands, Johnson Atoll, Midway Atoll, and several other Pacific islands.

In Florida, federal refuges include familiar names such as Pine Island, established 1908; Cedar Keys, 1929; St. Marks, 1931; J.N. "Ding" Darling, 1945; National Key Deer, 1954; Lake Woodruff, 1963; St. Vincent Island, 1968; Lower Suwannee, 1979; Crocodile Lake, 1979; Crystal River, 1983; Florida Panther, 1989; Archie Carr, 1991; Lake Wales Ridge, 1994; and Ten Thousand Islands, 1996.

How many species of wildlife have benefited from those protected havens of land, and how many people have grown to appreciate them? On Pelican Island, more than just brown and white pelicans use the island for roosting, nesting, and feeding. Other bird species include the double-crested cormorant, roseate spoonbill, wood stork, Forster's Tern, blue-wing teal, white ibis, American oystercatcher, anhinga, red-breasted merganser, ring-billed gull, and various egrets and herons. The Pelican Island Wildlife Festival, commemorating the birthday of Pelican Island and the National Wildlife Refuge System, is held every March. The 2022 festival featured a meet and greet with a Teddy Roosevelt impersonator.

The Pelican Island refuge—the first of its kind—may not have happened if it weren't for the determination of German immigrant Paul Kroegel In the late 1800s, before state or federal laws were enacted to protect nongame birds, Kroegel would sail out from his Sebastian house that was perched high atop an Ais Indian shell mound and stand guard on the island, gun in hand. He had had enough of watching birds slaughtered for their plume feathers, or simply shot for "fun" by passengers on passing steamboats.

A bald eagle calls along the Indian River Lagoon.

In 1901, Kroegel became one of four Florida wardens hired by the Florida Audubon Society (now Audubon of Florida) to protect birds. And after the island received its federal protection, he became its first manager. His initial salary: $1 a month.

But a presidential executive order still wasn't enough to protect Pelican Island. Commercial fishermen, viewing pelicans as a threat to their livelihood, were able to sneak onto the island in 1918 and club to death more than 400 defenseless pelican chicks. The threat abated after the Florida Audubon Society convinced the fishermen that pelicans primarily feed on noncommercial baitfish.

Mother Nature dealt the island a blow in 1923 when birds abandoned the island after a hurricane. Kroegel was soon retired from federal service, and the island was without a manager until the mid-1960s, even though many pelicans had returned.

The island was again threatened in the 1960s when developers sought to build on adjacent islands and wetlands. Local citizens, including commercial fishermen,

A boat travels through the Mosquito Lagoon.

citrus growers, and sportsmen, joined forces to form the Indian River Area Preservation League. They, along with Audubon of Florida, convinced the state to add 422 acres to the refuge. More land was acquired in the 1990s. The purchases allowed for a viewing tower to be built on adjacent land in 2003, marking the 100th anniversary of the refuge's establishment. The current refuge acreage is more than 5,400 acres.

Steps to the viewing tower are emblazoned with the names of each refuge within the national wildlife refuge system and the year they were established, reminding visitors that Pelican Island is more than an island with a few birds. As long as a piece of it still protrudes from the water, it stands as a testament to the time when the human species tempered its hard-driving temptation to destroy that which is defenseless and beautiful. The island marks a milestone for our species, and it gives us hope for our own survival.

Here's how Frank Chapman concludes his 1905 article about the island: "Man alone appears to threaten their continued existence, and from him, fortunately, those of their kin who live on Pelican Island are now happily protected. While they cannot repay their defenders with the music of thrushes or a display of those traits which so endear the higher animals to us, they may at least claim success in filling their place in nature, while the charm of every water-scene is increased by the quaint dignity of their presence."

From Pelican Island, many visitors enjoy the historic "jungle trail," an 8-mile-long sand road originally built in the 1920s for citrus growers. Today, one can drive the unpaved trail, but it is especially popular with pedestrians, joggers, and bicyclists. The path provides great views of the Indian River Lagoon and traverses some thick hammock areas of shady trees, thus the reason for its jungle name.

North of Pelican Island is the Costa Rica of small towns—Malabar—another prime example of humans preserving wildlife habitat. The community has protected 33 percent of its land area, or 6,447 acres, in some form of preservation. The conservation areas are connected by a variety of nonmotorized trails, a main reason Malabar was designated an official Florida trail town. It is just one more example why this section of coast is transforming into an ecotourism destination, one worthy of exploration.

11
ST. AUGUSTINE'S LIVING HISTORY

Colonial Quarter section of St. George Street in St. Augustine.

In visiting St. Augustine, the oldest European-founded city in the United States, you simply can't escape its historical nature. It literally surrounds you at every turn. It rubs on you, imbeds itself, whispers and shouts. From the gray coquina walls of Fort San Marcos to the carefully preserved buildings of St. George Street to the elaborate hotels of Henry Flagler's railroad empire, every era of St. Augustine's history is on display. It is no wonder this section of Florida's coast is known as the First Coast or Historic Coast.

Established in 1565 by Don Pedro Menendez de Aviles of Spain, St. Augustine has a distinct Spanish flavor since the city was Spain's Florida capital for more than two centuries, but maintaining Spanish rule was never easy. France, England, a young United States, and various Native American tribes also wrested for control of Florida through the historic town.

To protect the city, the Spanish built two forts in the area out of coquina rock, Fort Matanzas and Castillo de San Marcos. Most of the rock was mined on nearby Anastasia Island. The Spanish had good reason to build the forts since the English repeatedly raided St. Augustine, beginning in 1586 when Sir Francis Drake burned the city. Both forts are now national monuments open to the public.

Time and sun and tropical rains have exacted toll from crumbling parapets and gateways, stucco and paint have covered age-mellowed walls and antique planking, but much remains to preserve the charm and memories of an old city. . . . The Spanish flavor has remained dominant in the city's atmosphere as successive waves of non-Spanish settlers fell under its influence; climate, locations, and background have contributed to the preservation of its charm.

—*FLORIDA: A GUIDE TO THE SOUTHERNMOST STATE,*
FEDERAL WRITERS PROJECT, 1939

Water view and guard at Fort Matanzas National Monument.

Three cannon view at Fort Matanzas National Monument.

Fort Matanzas was built from 1740 to 1742 to guard the Matanzas Inlet, the southern coastal entrance to St. Augustine. The fort proved to be an adequate deterrent. Gunners fired upon British vessels soon after completion and never saw military action thereafter. It was likely a lonely existence for soldiers living in this isolated outpost.

To reach the fort today, visitors must take a ferry ride across the Matanzas Inlet, where they are often treated to a guided tour by a person in character as a Spanish infantryman. The panoramic view of a relatively unspoiled terrain from atop the fort is worth the trip alone. The fort site protects about 300 acres of Florida coastal habitat.

In touring the fort, individuals taller than 5 foot 7 must duck their heads through the doorways as most Spanish soldiers were smaller than average male adults today. Ground-shaking cannon-firing demonstrations periodically occur, so be sure to check the park's website for announcements.

The Castillo de San Marcos in St. Augustine, built over a 23-year time period beginning in 1672, is much larger than Fort Matanzas, and it saw more military action. During an English attack on St. Augustine in 1702, the fort was the only structure not captured.

During the Second Seminole War in 1837, Seminole Indian prisoners were housed in the "escape-proof" Spanish-built fort that the Americans called Fort Marion. On a night with little moonlight, the Seminoles chipped footholds and handholds in the stone wall of their cell with knives they had hidden. They wrenched free a rusty bar from the upper window and, having eaten little food for several weeks, managed to squeeze through the opening. The Seminole leader Wildcat later recalled the effort, "With much difficulty I succeeded in getting my head through; for the sharp stones took the skin off my breast and back." The Seminoles climbed down the outer stone walls using burlap feed bags tied together, sacks that had been given to them for their beds.

Although Castillo de San Marcos changed hands several times during its long history, the latest during the Civil War when both Confederate and Union forces occupied the fort, it was never taken by force. From 1875 to 1878, it was used to house 74 Plains Indian prisoners, and in the 1880s, more than 500 Apache Indians were imprisoned there. To these prisoners, far from their homes and perched on the vast Atlantic Ocean, life must have seemed bleak. Attempts were made to assimilate the prisoners into American society, and many of the Apache children were sent to the newly formed Carlisle Indian School in Pennsylvania. Some of the prisoners obviously clung to their traditional ways as evidenced by etchings in the stone walls of a Kiowa Sun Dance camp scene and an Apache Fire Dancer.

One other fort was built to protect St. Augustine, but the log structure no longer stands. Gracia Real de Santa Teresa de Mose, or Fort Mose, was the first legally sanctioned free black settlement in North America. Built in 1738, it served to protect the outer northern defenses of the city. The fort's initial occupants were runaways from English plantations in Carolina who were granted freedom in return for their service to the Spanish king and conversion to the Catholic faith. The deal

Fort Castillo de San Marcos has withstood battles and storms since the late 1600s.

paid off for Spain. Not only did it subvert slave labor in English colonies to the north, but the black troops also joined with Spanish regulars in driving off English invaders and their Native American allies in 1740. Two years later, they were also active in a Spanish counteroffensive against Georgia.

According to centuries-old historic documents, Fort Mose's village in 1759 consisted of 22 palm-thatched huts that housed 15 women, seven boys, eight girls, and 37 men, along with a wood church. The villagers married each other or enslaved people in St. Augustine, but a few men married Native American women. The inhabitants spoke several European and indigenous languages, and they displayed a variety of subsistence and artistic skills. The fort's lifespan proved to be short-lived, however. The inhabitants were forced to migrate to Spanish Cuba when Spain ceded Florida to England in 1763. The only other example of its kind in Florida history was when free black people, escaped slaves, and Native Americans took over a former British fort on the Apalachicola River in 1815.

Today, the site of Fort Mose is a state park that features a state-of-the-art visitor center and periodic cannon-firing demonstrations with volunteer reenactors.

But old Spanish military forts are only a few of the things to check out along the First Coast. In downtown St. Augustine, there is the oldest house and oldest schoolhouse attractions, an old jail, the oldest Catholic church in Florida, a pirate and treasure museum, a wax museum, Ripley's Believe It or Not, the "original" fountain of youth, the Governor's House Cultural Center and Museum, the Accord Civil Rights Museum that chronicles the local struggle to gain equal rights in the 1960s—as rough as any in the country—and the Colonial Quarter where

Reenactors load a cannon at Fort Mose Historic State Park.

blacksmiths, musketeers, and other demonstrators bring the 18th century to life. It is here where I watched a Spanish flamenco dancer intensely perform her traditional craft to an admiring private group who had booked the spot for dinner. There is also the Florida School of the Deaf and Blind, established in 1885; its most famous alumnus is singer Ray Charles.

Of course, downtown has plenty of kitsch to go around with gift shops on each block, and plenty of good restaurants ranging from the higher end Columbia to competing pizza parlors nearly facing off with each other on St. George Street. There are plenty of historic-looking pubs and taverns, too. One can see all of these attractions and more on foot since some streets are closed to vehicular traffic and there are ample sidewalks. Or, one can purchase a seat on an entertaining and informative open air tram ride or, even better, sit in a horse-drawn carriage and hear the clopping of hooves on cobblestone streets that have been part of the St. Augustine experience for centuries.

St. Augustine is also the site of two of railroad magnate Henry Flagler's original hotels. The Ponce de Leon is now part of Flagler College, and tours are available. The entrance features a solid gold dome. The cafeteria, once the hotel dining hall, boasts the largest collection of Tiffany-designed stained glass in the United States. Across the street, the former Alcazar Hotel is now the Lightsey Museum. Both hotels were elaborate for the day and catered to well-heeled Victorian tourists, but the Ponce de Leon Hotel was for upper-crust visitors who wanted to mingle with Henry Flagler himself during his visits. St. Augustine during the Gilded Age has been called Florida's first theme park—largely for upper-crust tourists—due to Flagler's influence.

On one visit to the former Ponce de Leon Hotel, I was taking photos in the ornate gold-domed rotunda when a distinguished-looking gentleman approached. He introduced himself as a professor at the college and asked, out of the blue, if I would like to see a floor tile that looked like Henry Flagler. Intrigued, I indicated I did. "It was placed there by workers as a kind of inside joke," he said. There were thousands of floor tiles, but this man slowly followed the patterns to a side hallway and abruptly stopped. "There, there it is," he said. And the tile did bear a resemblance to the hotel's founder.

Another St. Augustine surprise occurred in the Pirate & Treasure Museum across from the fort. I was on a group tour, and the long-haired, bearded guide was dressed as an 18th-century pirate with an ornate tricorn hat, loose red and black clothing, shoulder bag, hilted sword, and lots of jewelry. Staying in character the whole time, he had the brogue of someone who had sailed the high seas, and he spoke of the exhibits as if he had personally lived the adventures. By tour's end, I looked at the faces in our group and knew we were collectively wondering if this guy really was a pirate. Never had a living history interpreter been so convincing.

Of course, living history takes on a whole new meaning when it comes to the ever-popular St. Augustine ghost tours. Several companies offer evening tours, ranging from 90-minute walking tours to open-air tram rides to air-conditioned vans. Some tour guides even take on the persona of long dead prominent leaders in St. Augustine history with hopes that tour participants will meet the real personalities in ghostly form!

With all the goings-on in St. Augustine, it's fun to pause along one of the city's historic streets or in the main city plaza and reflect on both the generations of historic happenings and its march of visitors through the ages, some of whom had a measure of fame in their day. The poet Sidney Lanier was one of those, visiting the city in the early 1870s and becoming enraptured by the weather and gentle breezes of an April day: "And it is breathed always as it does on the day of this present writing—a sweet and saintly wind that is more soothing than a calm could be—one finds no difficulty in believing that in the course of a few years the entire population of the earth and of the heavens above the earth and of the waters beneath the earth would be settled in and around this quaint, romantic, straggling, dear and dearer-growing city of St. Augustine."

Fortunately, Lanier was prone to hyperbole. The 2020 population of St. Augustine was under 15,000, although tourism numbers easily dwarf the number of year-round residents, typically exceeding five million a year. At one time, a visit to St. Augustine was considered a side trip on the way to Orlando theme parks, but almost three-quarters of today's visitors are viewing St. Augustine as their primary destination, staying multiple nights. This has helped boost a new industry—heritage tourism. Instead of relegating history to signs, books, and the occasional museum like in many towns, St. Augustine puts it front and center for visitors. And if history isn't enough, coastal natural areas abound in the St. Augustine region, luring outdoor lovers.

The public pier at Vilano Beach across the Intracoastal Waterway from St. Augustine.

To the northeast, just past the idyllic coastal village of Vilano Beach, a natural area with the world's longest name offers miles of hiking trails and a protected waterway to explore—the Guana Tolomato Matanzas National Estuarine Research Reserve, one of 29 such reserves across the United States. The reserve protects 76,760 acres and an astounding number of plant and animal species.

To the southeast of St. Augustine, Anastasia Island State Park features miles of white sand beaches and a campground, just past the spiral striped St. Augustine Lighthouse, which is open for public touring. Much of the coquina rock used to build Castillo de San Marcos in St. Augustine was quarried on Anastasia Island by the Spanish. And nearby is the St. Augustine Alligator Farm Zoological Park. In the early 1890s, George Reddington and Felix Fire ran a tram from the city to Anastasia Island. They often had to stop and remove alligators from the tracks, and they noticed the excitement this caused among passengers. An idea formed. They captured a few gators and put them in a bathhouse on the beach and charged customers a quarter to see them. The longest-surviving alligator attraction in the country was born. It now features zip lines and examples of every crocodilian species found in the world. It is also a great place to see hundreds of nesting wading birds, especially in spring, since they are attracted to large congregations of alligators that protect them from climbing predators such as raccoons.

A must-stop on any tour of this coast is Washington Oaks Gardens State Park, once owned by a relative of George Washington. The creator of the gardens along the Matanzas River envisioned a manicured exotic landscape "in the jungle" with

Visitors explore the unique coquina rocks at Washington Oaks Gardens State Park.

numerous fountains and reflective pools, and they succeeded in carrying out this vision of loveliness. Two-hundred-year-old live oaks with their arching limbs festooned with Spanish moss and resurrection ferns provide a natural garden dome. Not surprisingly, the hill at the top of the rose garden is an ancient Native American shell midden.

Equally impressive as the gardens is the beach portion of this state park along the Atlantic shore since it features unique coquina rock formations where one can investigate small grottos and tidal pools rich in marine life.

Interestingly, during the many times the Washington Oaks property changed hands since the early 1800s, it was sold to a developer in 1923 and was to become a new subdivision known as Hernandez Estates, named after its first owner, Jose Hernandez. Hernandez was a St. Augustine native who became a brigadier general in the Second Seminole War and was partly responsible for the shameful capturing of Osceola and other Seminole leaders under a flag of truce. The collapse of the Florida land boom iced the development project, and finally, in 1964, then owner Louise Young donated the land to the state, specifying that the gardens be "maintained in their present form."

Other nature parks in the region include Faver-Dykes State Park on scenic Pellicer Creek; Gamble Rogers Memorial State Recreation Area at Flagler Beach, named after a famous Florida folk singer who sacrificed his life trying to rescue a swimmer in distress; and Princess Place Preserve, named after a former owner who married an exiled Russian prince.

At Bulow Plantation Ruins Historic State Park, accessed by the long, canopied "beach road" once used by carriages, moss-covered stone ruins of a sugar mill resemble a hollowed-out medieval castle. The plantation buildings were burned by raiding Seminole Indians in 1836. And at nearby Tomoka State Park, site of the Timucuan village of Nocoroco described by the Spanish in 1605, one can gaze upon the curious 45-foot statue called the *Legend of Tomokie*. Created by artist Frederick Dana Marsh in 1955, the legend and depiction is considered fictional, the statue being a prime example of Florida outdoor folk art.

One of Florida's first 20th-century theme parks still attracts visitors along Highway A1A south of St. Augustine. Marineland was the world's first "oceanarium" where a host of marine creatures would swim together in large tanks that simulated a natural environment. Opened in 1938 as "Marine Studios" by an eclectic group that included members of the Vanderbilt and Tolstoy families, the attraction began as an underwater film studio where portions of several movies were filmed, including *Creature from the Black Lagoon* (1954) and *Revenge of the Creature* (1955). Cameras could easily film into the tanks through glass portholes.

Several breakthroughs regarding captive dolphins occurred at Marineland, including the first study of dolphin echolocation and the first dolphin birth in captivity, a calf named Spray. Also, in the late 1940s, animal keepers noticed how dolphins would often jump for their rations of fish and so an idea was born. Why not train the dolphins to jump for fish and do other tricks for an adoring public? The famous aerial dolphin acts were born.

Eventually, Marineland fell on hard times with the advent of central Florida's gargantuan theme parks, especially Sea World, followed by damaging hurricanes. The facility has since been revived, with a special emphasis on dolphin interactions. One room in the attraction serves as a small museum, helping visitors appreciate its colorful past and elevating Marineland as one more historical jewel along Florida's First Coast.

A pair of leaping dolphins entertain visitors at Marineland.

An osprey scans Florida coastal waters for its next meal.

Route A1A leaves the continent of North America at the northeastern tip of Florida, heading east. It aims toward a particular sea island like a concrete finger, pointing the way across a great plain of dense, broad puffs of marsh cordgrass, grouted with brown ribbons of mud. Midway over the wide green labyrinth, A1A arches high above the sinuous Amelia River, as it snakes its way through the tidal wetlands. Just beyond the swath of blue, the road dips to meet a second marsh meadow, a carpet of cordgrass laid before an island named for a princess. Here can first be felt the call of Amelia.

—DEON LAWRANCE JACCARD,
THE HISTORIC SPLENDOR OF AMELIA ISLAND 1997

BLUFFS AND TIDAL MAZES

Like St. Augustine, one can live and breathe a rich history along the northernmost stretch of Florida's east coast. There are plantation houses, Civil War–era forts, and pubs still serving suds for more than a century. Even the geographic names are historic. Amelia Island, for example, was named for the daughter of England's King George II in 1735 while the region was still under Spanish rule, and Fernandina Beach—also known as Fernandina and Old Fernandina—was platted and named after King Ferdinand VII of Spain in 1811. It was Spain's last attempt at New World town building. For these reasons and more, this stretch of coast running from Jacksonville to Georgia's Cumberland Island is still part of the First Coast or Historic Coast. It also uniquely boasts unspoiled public lands, mazes of tidal creeks, coastal bluffs, and numerous sea islands.

The largest population center is the City of Jacksonville with more than a million residents. Chartered in 1832 and named after Andrew Jackson, Florida's first territorial governor, Jacksonville has long been an important seaport. The city figured prominently in the Civil War, being occupied by Union forces on four separate occasions. In 1901, a devastating fire, dwarfed only by the Great Chicago Fire and the 1906 San Francisco Earthquake, left thousands homeless, but the city was quickly rebuilt. Eventually, Jacksonville merged with Duval County, making it the largest city by landmass in the United States and one that boasts 22 miles of oceanfront beaches.

Just to the north is the historic American Beach, once an ocean retreat for African Americans during Jim Crow days. Opened in 1935 by A. L. Lewis, who bought 200 acres for his insurance company employees with the motto of "Recreation and Relaxation without Humiliation," American Beach is marked by state historical signs today and is largely bordered by gated resort communities. The Trust for Public Land has purchased the Evanses' Rendezvous nightclub site at American Beach and is working with Nassau County to restore the building and several nearby sites. There is also the A. L. Lewis Museum open Friday through Sunday. A unique natural feature of American Beach is a dune system dubbed "Nana" by the late MaVynee Betsch, also known as the "Beach Lady" and a strong advocate for preservation of the area. The 60-foot dune, the tallest in Florida, is now part of the Timucuan Ecological and Historic Preserve.

African Americans also used a segregated beach at Little Talbot Island State Park, thus the reason there are two separate beach parking areas in the park today. African American beaches were found throughout Florida during Jim Crow days, often established only after determined efforts by those shut out of "whites only" public beaches. Besides beaches, *The Negro Travelers' Green Book*, published between 1936 and 1967, was an essential guide for African American travelers in finding safe accommodations and restaurants. Of the 47 sites listed for Florida in the 1959 guide, 10 were for Jacksonville, the largest number of any Florida town or city.

Surprisingly, if traveling along the Atlantic shore in Duval County, Jacksonville's urban reaches are negligible. That's because most of its industrial development has been along the lower St. Johns River and Intracoastal Waterway. Plus, as a way to offset and prevent urban sprawl, vast stretches of marsh, islands, and coastal forest have been protected largely through the efforts of the City of Jacksonville, the Timucuan National Preserve, and private landowners and nonprofit groups.

In 1999, then mayor John Delaney spearheaded Preservation Project Jacksonville. He encouraged voters to approve a $300 million bond issue to protect choice parcels of Jacksonville's remaining undeveloped land, making Jacksonville a national leader in terms of protected park acreage. Delaney said the idea—or epiphany—came to him while fishing.

"We can use taxpayer money in one of two ways," he said in unveiling his plan. "We can either expand our roadways, which will only encourage uncontrolled growth and create 12-lane parking lots on our roadways. Or we can have the vision to preserve large tracts of land now and give our citizens the opportunity to experience these unspoiled natural greenspaces. When faced with the option of a generic strip mall on every corner or a beautiful green park for families to enjoy, I think the choice is a natural one."

Since then, more than 51,000 acres have been protected. The goal is to help guide growth, protect environmentally sensitive lands, improve water quality, and provide more outdoor recreation opportunities. The result has been a ring of protected lands and wetlands around the city, much of it being coastal habitat. And part of the city's current vision is to link many of these areas by way of multiuse trails so much of the city's population can access wild beauty without the need for a vehicle. Florida author Marjorie Kinnan Rawlings once said, "I do not know how anyone can live without some small place of enchantment to turn to."

Federal lands along this stretch of coast include the 46,000-acre Timucuan Ecological and Historic Preserve, named after the Timucua people who occupied these lands and waters and who were wiped out by warfare and disease by 1800. One can't go too far into the preserve's vast wetlands and sea islands without bumping into early historical sites. An example is the Fort Caroline National Memorial near the mouth of the St. Johns River, a reconstructed 16th-century fort that acknowledges the short-lived French occupation in Florida. The settlement was as much a religious occupation as a military and economic one since French Protestants known as Huguenots came to the New World to escape persecution.

The Fort Caroline National Memorial just north of Jacksonville marks a short-lived French occupation along the Florida coast.

Spain—an age-old adversary—was uneasy about the French presence, fearing their treasure ships sailing up the Gulf Stream en route to Spain with Mexican and Peruvian gold would be easy prey. In 1565, Admiral Pedro Menendez was given the assignment to eliminate the French presence. It proved easier than anticipated. French naval officer Jean Ribault embarked a preemptive strike by sailing down the coast to attack the new village of St. Augustine only to confront a hurricane instead. Consequently, his fleet was scattered and wrecked about 15 miles south. Seizing an opportunity, Menendez first proceeded to wipe out the lightly guarded Fort Caroline with 500 soldiers. He then sailed south to confront Ribault's scattered forces. Ribault and his soldiers surrendered, but Menendez cruelly put them to the sword. They were French, after all, long-time enemies—and most were Protestants. Only a few Catholics in the group were spared. The place of the massacre became known as Matanzas, Spanish for slaughters. The French never again posed a serious threat to Spanish rule in Florida.

Eventually, mostly English and American aristocrats built large plantations on Fort George and Amelia Islands in the 1700s and 1800s. Cash crops included Sea Island cotton—known for its long, silky fiber—and indigo, which produced a highly prized blue dye. Food crops such as okra, beans, sugar cane, potatoes, yams, peas, eggplant, and squash were also grown to feed the planter's families and enslaved occupants.

Carefully preserved buildings of the Kingsley Plantation, part of the Timucuan Ecological and Historic Preserve.

The remains of slave cabins on the Kingsley Plantation built from a unique type of concrete known as tabby.

Original buildings that were part of the Kingsley Plantation have been carefully preserved by the National Park Service. The plantation house, built in 1798 by Zephaniah Kingsley, is the oldest surviving structure of its kind in Florida. The plantation is located along the Fort George River on a 1,000-acre island, only 2 miles inland from the Atlantic Ocean. The ocean's close proximity helped the plantation ship goods and receive supplies. Today, visitors can view the planter's residence, kitchen, and barn along with the ghostly husks of slave quarters made from tabby—a type of concrete composed of lime from burned oyster shells mixed with water, sand, ash, and shells. The shells were often taken from shell mounds or middens conveniently left on the island by countless generations of Timucuan Indians and their ancestors. The fact that remnants of 25 slave houses still stand speaks to the durability of this early coastal building material and the ingenuity of its creators. The cabins are in an arc or semicircle similar to those found in some West African villages.

The Kingsley family was unique in that Zephaniah Kingsley took an African wife, Anna, and they had several children together while she was still in her teens. He decided to free his family in 1811 in a formal "Manumission Document": "In the name of Almighty God, Amen: Let it be known that I, Zephaniah Kingsley, resident and citizen of the St. Johns River region of this province hereby state: That I have as my slave a black woman named Anna, about 18 years old, who is the same native African woman that I purchased in Havana . . . I recognize [her children] as my own; this circumstance, and as well considering the good qualities of the already referred to black woman, and the truth and fidelity with which she has served me, impels me to give her freedom graciously and without other interest, the same accorded to the aforementioned three mulatto children whose names and ages are for the record: George, three years and nine months old; Martha, twenty months old; and Mary, a month old."

Besides becoming a business partner with her husband, Anna Kingsley eventually owned her own plantation and slaves, taking advantage of more liberal Spanish laws regarding free people of color. Zephaniah Kingsley was no abolitionist, but after Spain sold Florida to the United States in 1821, he put forth to the state's new political leaders that people should be judged by class, not by color. He underlined the importance of a free black population in Florida and that those in slavery should be treated justly with "a patriarchal feeling of affection." His arguments went unheeded. Harsher restrictions were enacted regarding free and enslaved people in Florida, and by 1837, most of the Kingsley family and 50 newly freed slaves moved to Haiti, a free black colony. Two daughters, however, remained in Florida, having married wealthy white men in Jacksonville.

In Fernandina Beach on Amelia Island, an impressive 50 blocks of this historic town are listed in the National Register of Historic Places. Visitors can stroll along the streets and check out the charming Victorian architecture of the late 1800s. And the town lays claim to the oldest operating bar in Florida, having a one-up on St. Augustine.

A look inside the historic Palace Saloon in Fernandina Beach.

The Palace Saloon opened in 1903 and was considered a true "gentleman's establishment" and "ship captain's bar" with complimentary towels to wipe foam from patrons' mustaches. Guests included members of the Carnegie family from nearby Cumberland Island. The saloon survived Prohibition by selling cigars, special wines, 3 percent near-beer, and gasoline. According to the Palace website, the saloon "still has the elegant features that made it famous for over a century: inlaid mosaic floors, embossed tin ceilings, hand-carved mahogany caryatides (undraped female fixtures), a 40-foot bar lit with gas lamps, and walls painted with six commissioned murals. . . . Go ahead, belly up to the bar, and as the bartender slides a mug of suds to you, the ghosts from ten decades past join in drinking to your health."

In the spring, Fernandina Beach hosts the Isle of Eight Flags Shrimp Festival, which celebrates the town's shrimp industry and the eight flags that have flown over Amelia Island—more than any other spot in the United States. Since the 1500s, the flags have been French, Spanish, English, Patriots, Green Cross of Florida, Mexican, Confederate, and United States. The Patriots, Green Cross, and Mexican flags belonged to local groups who seized control of the island for brief periods in the early 1800s.

Another Fernandina Beach festival celebrates an annual event of a different kind—the North Atlantic right whale calving season that begins in mid-November and runs through mid-April. The free two-day event occurs every November at the main beach and raises awareness about the plight of this highly endangered whale. Florida whale watchers are generally on the lookout for right whales from Fernandina to Cape Canaveral with February being the prime whale-watching month. Long fishing piers make for good whale-watching posts. Since hunting has been banned since 1949, the primary causes of right whale death involve collisions with ships and entanglements in fishing gear. Most adult right whales are about 50 feet long and weigh up to 70 tons. They often breach and tail slap and can swim fairly close to shore.

Fernandina Beach is also known for being the eastern terminus of the first Atlantic to Gulf Railroad. Spearheaded by David Levy Yulee and finished just weeks before cannons roared at Fort Sumter to begin the Civil War, the railroad stretched to Cedar Key, creating a direct route for trade that previously had to go by ship around the Florida Keys. Yulee served two terms as a US senator from Florida and was the first person of Jewish ancestry to serve in the Senate. During the war, he was prosecession from the Union and, after the war, served several months in prison for aiding in the escape of Confederate president Jefferson Davis. While Yulee's original railroad is defunct, Fernandina Beach still has an active rail line that services two large pulp mills.

The northern terminus of Florida's Atlantic Coast is Fort Clinch, another coastal fort with a long history and now part of a Florida state park. Construction of fortifications at this strategic location along Cumberland Sound and the St. Mary's River began in 1736, but it wasn't until 1847 when construction of the larger fort that we see today—mostly red brick and mortar—began in earnest. During the Civil War, the fort was first occupied by Confederate troops, but a strategic withdrawal occurred in March 1862 due to the growing strength of Union forces along the Georgia coast. Union troops then took control. The fort was abandoned in 1869 until the Spanish-American War when it was briefly revived as a barracks and ammunition depot. Then it was abandoned again. The army sold the fort to private entities in 1926, but concerned citizens stepped in and were successful in establishing Fort Clinch State Park in 1935, one of the state's first. The Civilian Conservation Corps was instrumental in restoring the fort and building a museum, campground, and access roads. The fort briefly served as a joint military operations center for surveillance and communications during World War II before being returned to state management. Today, visitors can tour the fort daily

An American flag flies at Fort Clinch along Cumberland Sound.

and witness periodic reenactments and living history demonstrations by volunteers, especially on the first Saturday of each month.

Nature lovers can also enjoy Fort Clinch State Park's hiking trails along sand beaches and beneath old-growth live oaks with their complementary Spanish moss, resurrection fern, and bromeliads. If ambitious, one can ride bicycles south almost 17 miles on the Amelia Island and Timucuan paved multiuse trails, now part of the 3,000-mile East Coast Greenway being developed from Maine to Key West. The trails link three other premier state parks to the south—Amelia Island, Big Talbot, and Little Talbot, all of which boast pristine Atlantic beaches. Amelia Island State Park is the only Florida state park that offers horseback riding on its beaches, and there are low bluffs at Big Talbot where the relentless sea is pushing inland on a scenic coastal live oak forest and leaving behind a ghost forest of bleached trees along the shore.

One beach on Big Talbot is known as Blackrock where Simpson's Creek begins emptying into the Atlantic. There are only 15 parking spaces to access the beach, so if you are one of the lucky few to park and hike the half mile to the beach at low tide, you will be greeted by a stretch of gleaming black shoreline interspersed with patches of bright green seaweed. It is a scene reminiscent of a Hawaiian volcanic beach, even though the "rocks" on this Florida beach largely consist of dark soil hardened and bisected by the elements.

Bicyclist on the Amelia Island Trail through Little Talbot State Park.

The wild coastal forest of Big Talbot Island State Park.

Blackrock Beach on Big Talbot Island State Park.

Looking toward the mouth of Simpson's Creek where it meets the Atlantic, the undeveloped shore meanders in and out of a bay and around a peninsula, framed by saw palmetto, live oak, and cedar. The urge to explore is irresistible for this is how all of Florida's coast once looked—wild and untamed, stretching more than 1,000 miles through a myriad of habitats and past dozens of river outlets, islands, and bays. It is Florida, unmatched, a synergy of sun, sand, and surf that continues to draw not only people but also marine animals ranging from sea turtles to horseshoe crabs. And it will continue as long as we are vigilant in its care.

Downed windswept palms along the beach of Little Talbot Island State Park. Downed trees are kept in place because they help protect the living coastal forest from storm surge.

Group picking up trash on a spoil island along Apalachicola Bay.

Coastal fortification without development policy changes will simply encourage even more construction in vulnerable coastal zones, creating even more future stranded assets. What is really needed is for Florida to adopt the full range of transformations in energy and development, changes that will not only slow climate change but will also yield benefits to water quality, wildlife, and quality of life.

—JOHN C. CAPECE, PHD, KISSIMMEE WATERKEEPER, 2021

Florida has more than 1,260 miles of coastline—more coastline than any other state in the continental United States. Given our vulnerability to hurricanes and flooding, where's the most dangerous place to live? The coast. Yet where do most of us live? The coast. And where's the one place you can get taxpayer-subsidized flood insurance? The coast.

—CRAIG PITTMAN, *OH, FLORIDA!*, 2017

I'm optimistic. I think we can pass from conquerors to stewards.

—E. O. WILSON, 2012

13

HELPING
OUR COAST

It might be the thrill of seeing a sea turtle or dolphin break a placid surface, a diving osprey or pelican, or the rare breach of a whale or manta ray or school of flying fish. Perhaps it is the breathtaking sunrises and sunsets that cast lavender colors across water and sand, bathing all in its path. Maybe it is the feel of warm sand on feet and body and the steady, soothing mantra of breaking waves. It might be the thrill of hooking a tarpon or other fighting fish or gathering scallops across the sea floor that hearkens back to a hunter-gatherer era.

It is usually a special moment that begins a relationship with Florida's coast, one that can grow over a lifetime. And as with any close relationship, we can become concerned when something is amiss. It might be coastal development, harmful algal blooms, a die-off of marine life, or rising sea levels. So, what can we do?

To make a difference in protecting Florida's coast, concerted efforts must be made from all facets of society. Coastal threats impact not only marine life but also a huge portion of our tourist-oriented economy. So, concerned citizens can enlist the support of businesses, chambers of commerce, tourist development councils, and civic groups. No one wants to see pollution or flooded communities, but addressing the root cause of problems takes political will, funding, and scientific-based guidance. Politicians will only lead if the people compel them to lead.

One thing that brings people together are coastal cleanups, cleaning up those natural areas we love. And they are important. Trash such as styrofoam and plastics never goes away; it only gets smaller and smaller and can be ingested by birds, turtles, and marine mammals, acting like plankton floating in our waterways. These particles cannot be digested and can eventually cause death. And some coastal cleanups, known as ghost trap rodeos, coordinated by Ocean Aid 360, involve removing abandoned and lost crab traps that can continue to entrap marine life.

Cleanups can be done solo, but there is something special about working with others for a common good and the satisfaction of stepping back afterward and scanning eyes over a trash-free waterfront view. As one cleanup participant observed, "Who knew garbage pickup could be so fun!"

There are several other ways you can help our oceans and coast:

- Use environmentally friendly cleaning, household, and lawn products. Chemicals that go down our drains and toilets, or are spread on our lawns, can end up in waterways and can eventually flow into the oceans.
- Consider the source of products that come from the oceans, such as seafood, aquarium fish, coral, and shells. How were these products harvested? Do the countries of origin have management plans that ensure the long-term conservation of the species?
- Buy organic foods because organic farmers do not use pesticides and chemical fertilizers that can pollute waterways and oceans.
- Promote energy efficiency and clean, renewable energy that can reduce the harmful effects of global warming on phytoplankton, coral reefs, and other marine environments.
- Phase out offshore oil drilling. The 2010 Deepwater Horizon Spill of 4.9 million barrels of oil was the worst man-made disaster in Gulf Coast history. The long-term effects of the spill on marine life are still being measured.
- Reduce, reuse, and recycle products, especially plastics, to eliminate litter that might end up in the oceans, and participate in coastal cleanups.
- Do not support cruise lines that dump waste of any kind into the oceans.
- Support aquariums and other facilities that rescue injured marine life and shore birds and help rehabilitate them.
- Follow steps during turtle nesting season such as turning off or shading all lights visible from the beach and pulling all furniture away from the beach at night.
- Support marine conservation organizations and learn about ways you can help our oceans through contributions and volunteer work.
- Promote sensible building restrictions in hurricane-prone areas along with the protection of ecologically rich coastal properties.
- Volunteer to replant sea oats on dunes, monitor sea turtle nests, and do other worthwhile projects.

In working to protect our coast and marine life, there are occasional moments to celebrate when things can initially look dire. In October 2021, during a severe red tide outbreak on St. George Island, Franklin County sheriff's deputies picked up a lethargic and severely dehydrated adult loggerhead sea turtle and brought it to Gulf Specimen Marine Lab in Panacea. Turtles absorb the red tide neurotoxins through their skin and by eating infected organisms and can essentially become paralyzed. The attending staff and volunteer vet at the marine lab had little hope the female loggerhead would make it through the night. "As we picked her up, she went completely limp," said lab manager Cypress Rudloe. "So, she had no movement in her flippers. She couldn't keep her head up." But after gallons of IV fluids, the turtle began to show signs of recovery. The staff named her Hope, and her plight captured the hearts of many.

Hope the loggerhead sea turtle heading to sea on St. George Island with a large crowd looking on.

After months of feeding, resting, and swimming in one of the aquarium's large tanks, Hope was ready to be returned to the ocean. On a cool January afternoon, hundreds of people of all ages gathered on the St. George Island beach—sans red tide—for Hope's release. The 150-pound turtle was carried to the shore in a sling by members of the Gulf Specimen staff and the sheriff's deputies who had rescued her. Cameras and cell phones were held high as Hope was laid on the sand. She did not hesitate! Hope began to vigorously crawl toward the water, shepherded by Gulf Specimen cofounder Jack Rudloe in the blue suit he traditionally wears for turtle releases. Cheers erupted as she entered the surf and slowly disappeared beneath waves, free again to roam the seas. It was a festive event and, rightfully, one filled with hope since so many people obviously cared about Hope's recovery. It illustrated how Florida's coast—and its creatures—was larger than any one person or any one generation. It spans all of Florida's human evolution, and it is dynamic and changing.

Much has been destroyed or altered, but some places have been carefully protected and even restored, and some sea creatures such as sea turtles are actually gaining in numbers, leading the way for how it can be done elsewhere. It is up to us to help protect and maintain what makes our coast special.

BIBLIOGRAPHY

Adair Realty and Trust. "Profits Reward the Pioneer: Whitfield Estates on Sarasota Bay." *Suniland Magazine*, November 1925.

Akin, Edward N. *Flagler: Rockefeller Partner and Florida Baron*. Gainesville: University Press of Florida, 1992.

Alderson, Doug. "Florida's Ambitious Circumnavigational Trail Challenges, Thrills." *Tallahassee Democrat*. March 16, 2019.

———. *Nostalgic Florida: Iconic Village Art of the Sunshine State*. Palm Beach, FL: Pineapple Press, 2022.

———. *Wild Florida Waters: Exploring the Sunshine State by Kayak and Canoe*. Seattle: CreateSpace Independent Publishing Platform, 2011.

Barbour, George M. *Florida for Tourists, Invalids, and Settlers*. New York: Appleton, 1882.

Bickel, Karl A. *The Mangrove Coast: The Story of the West Coast of Florida*. New York: Coward McCann, 1942.

Biscayne National Park. "Birth of Biscayne National Park." National Park Service, accessed October 24, 2020. https://www.nps.gov/bisc/learn/historyculture/the-birth-of-biscayne-national-park.htm.

———. "The Joneses of Porgy Key." National Park Service, accessed December 13, 2021. https://home.nps.gov/bisc/learn/historyculture/the-joneses-of-porgy-key.htm.

Bishop, Nathaniel H. *Four Months in a Sneak-Box*. Boston: Lee and Shepard, 1879.

Blatchley, W. S. *My Nature Nook: Notes on the Natural History of the Vicinity of Dunedin, Florida*. Indianapolis, IN: Nature, 1931.

Brinkman, Paul. "Florida Makes Last-Ditch Effort to Save Its Oyster Capital." United Press International, August 24, 2020. https://www.upi.com/Top_News/US/2020/08/24/Florida-makes-last-ditch-effort-to-save-its-oyster-capital/1381597863339/.

Brown, Robin C. *Florida's First People*. Sarasota, FL: Pineapple Press, 1994.

Buker, George E. *Swamp Sailors: Riverine Warfare in the Everglades 1835–1842*. Gainesville: University Press of Florida, 1975.

Burgess, Robert F., and Carl J. Clausen. *Florida's Golden Galleons: The Search for the 1715 Spanish Treasure Fleet*. Port Salerno: Florida Classics Library, 1982.

Burlew, Jeff. "Hurricane Michael: 'Like a Bomb Went Off' in Jackson County, Marianna." *Tallahassee Democrat*, October 12, 2018.

Burt, Al. *Al Burt's Florida: Snowbirds, Sand Castles, and Self-Rising Crackers*. Gainesville: University Press of Florida, 1997.

Byrne, Stephanie, and Drew Hill. "Red Tide Reemerges in Southwest Florida." *WINK News*, October 18, 2021. https://www.winknews.com/2021/10/18/red-tide-reemerges-in-southwest-florida/.

Byron, Su. "Cortez Village: Yesterday and Today." YourObserver.com, February 20, 2020. https://www.yourobserver.com/article/cortez-village-yesterday-and-today.

Camp Gordon Johnston WWII Museum. "History of Camp Gordon Johnston." Accessed August 13, 2020. https://www.campgordonjohnston.com/learn/history-of-camp-gordon-johnston/.

Camp Helen State Park. "Camp Helen State Park History." Accessed July 30, 2020. https://www.floridastateparks.org/parks-and-trails/camp-helen-state-park/history.

Canaveral National Seashore. "Canaveral National Seashore." National Park Service, accessed December 21, 2021. https://www.nps.gov/cana/index.htm.

Carr, Archie. *So Excellent a Fishe: A Natural History of Sea Turtles*. Gainesville: University Press of Florida, 2011.

Cash, W. T. "Taylor County History and Civil War Deserters." *Florida Historical Quarterly* 26 (July 1947–April 1948): 28–49.

Castello, David J. "The Barefoot Mailman." West Palm Beach.com, accessed October 28, 2020. https://www.westpalmbeach.com/the-barefoot-mailman/.

Cedar Key Chamber of Commerce. "Life by the Sea." Accessed August 8, 2020. http://cedarkey.org/.

Cerulean, Susan. *Coming to Pass: Florida's Coastal Islands in a Gulf of Change*. Athens and London: University of Georgia Press, 2015.

Cerulean, Susan, Janisse Ray, and Laura Newton. *Between Two Rivers: Stories from the Red Hills to the Gulf*. Tallahassee, FL: Red Hills Writers Project, 2004.

Chapman, Frank M. "An Intimate Study of the Pelican." *The Century Magazine*, 1905. Reprinted in *Tales of Old Florida* by Castle Books in 1987.

Coastal Breeze News. "DEP Welcomes Everglades City as Florida Trail Town." February 15, 2019. https://www.coastalbreezenews.com/news/dep-welcomes-everglades-city-as-florida-trail-town/article_20b073f7-6525-595c-9b38-e4bb397a5cf7.html.

Connell, Vivian. "Mysterious Sidewalk Marks Bonita Beach." *Taco Times* (Perry, FL), July 10, 1985.

Davis, Jack E. *The Gulf: The Making of an American Sea*. New York and London: Liveright, 2017.

De Soto National Memorial. "History & Culture." National Park Service, accessed August 30, 2020. https://www.nps.gov/deso/learn/historyculture/index.htm.

De Vaca, Alvar Nunez Cabeza. *Adventures in the Unknown Interior of America*. Reprint, Albuquerque: University of New Mexico Press, 1983. Originally published 1542.

Deland, Margaret. *Florida Days*. Boston: Little, Brown, 1889.

Destin Chamber. "History of Destin and Its White Sand." Accessed July 29, 2020. https://www.destinchamber.com/history-of-destin.

Dickinson, Jonathan. *Jonathan Dickinson's Journal or God's Protecting Providence*. Stuart, FL: Valentine Books, 1975 edition of the 1699 journal.

Dimmock, A. W. *Florida Enchantments*. New York: Stokes, 1926.

Dodd, Dorothy. *Florida in the War, 1861–1865*. Tallahassee, FL: Peninsular Publishing, 1959.

———. "The Wrecking Business on the Florida Reef 1822–1860." *Florida Historical Quarterly* 14, no. 4 (April 1944): 171–99.

Douglas, Marjory Stoneman. *The Everglades: River of Grass*. New York: Rinehart, 1947.

Dumitrascu, Sarah. "Marineland: The History of Bringing the Ocean Ashore." *The Jaxson* (Jacksonville, FL), June 23, 2021.

Dunn, Hampton. "David Levy Yulee: Florida's First U.S. Senator." *Sunland Tribune* 21, no. 1 (1995): article 7. https://scholarcommons.usf.edu/sunlandtribune/vol21/iss1/7.

Egmont Key State Park. "History of Egmont Key." Florida State Parks, accessed August 30, 2020. https://www.floridastateparks.org/learn/history-egmont-key.

Eidse, Faith. *Voices of the Apalachicola.* Gainesville: University Press of Florida, 2006.

Farrington, Brendan. "Florida Lighthouse Lost to the Sea Now Stands Again." *USA Today*, July 28, 2008. http://www.usatoday.com/travel/destinations/2008-07-28-cape-st-george-lighthouse_N.htm.

Fishburne, Charles Carroll, Jr. *The Cedar Keys in the Nineteenth Century.* Cedar Key, FL: Cedar Key Historical Society, 1997.

Fisher, Jerry M. *The Pacesetter: The Untold Story of Carl G. Fisher.* Fort Bragg, CA: Lost Coast Press, 1998.

Florida Fish and Wildlife Conservation Commission. "Sea Turtles." Accessed December 23, 2021. https://myfwc.com/research/wildlife/sea-turtles/.

———. "Tarpon Facts." Accessed September 27, 2020. https://myfwc.com/research/saltwater/tarpon/information/facts/#:~:text=Tarpon%20can%20reach%20sizes%20up,is%20nicknamed%20%22silver%20king.%22.

Florida Museum. "Fort Mose: America's Black Colonial Fortress of Freedom." Accessed December 30, 2021. https://www.floridamuseum.ufl.edu/histarch/research/st-augustine/fort-mose/.

Fort Clinch State Park. "History of Fort Clinch." Florida State Parks, accessed January 24, 2022. https://www.floridastateparks.org/learn/history-fort-clinch.

Fox, Charles Donald. *The Truth about Florida.* New York: Renard, 1925.

Friends of Washington Oaks Gardens State Park. "History of Washington Oaks Gardens State Park." Accessed December 31, 2021. http://www.washingtonoaks.org/history.html.

Gallagher, Peter B. "Emateloye Estenletkvte: Polly Parker Got Away." *Seminole Tribune*, December 17, 2013.

Green, Alma D., ed. *The Negro Travelers' Green Book 1959 Edition.* New York: Victor H. Green, 1959. Facsimile ed., Orlando, FL: About Comics, 2022.

Green, Ben. *Finest Kind: A Celebration of a Florida Fishing Village.* Macon, GA: Mercer University Press, 1985.

Greenberg, Margaret H. *Nature on Sanibel.* Ocoee, FL: Anna Publishing, 1985.

Gross, Bonnie. "Whale Watching in Florida: Winter Thrill on Northeast Coast." Florida Rambler, March 4, 2022, accessed April 10, 2022. https://www.floridarambler.com/northeast-florida-getaways/right-whale-watching-in-florida/.

Hammond, John Martin. *Winter Journeys in the South.* Philadelphia and London: Lippincott, 1916.

Harrison, Carlos. "Top Nude Beaches in Florida." Visit Florida, accessed January 31, 2022. https://www.visitflorida.com/beaches/faq/nude-beaches/.

Hill, Drew. "Red Tide Reemerges in Southwest Florida." WINK News, October 18, 2021. https://www.winknews.com/2021/10/18/red-tide-reemerges-in-southwest-florida/.

Hiller, Herb. *Highway A1A: Florida at the Edge.* Gainesville: University Press of Florida, 2005.

———. "South Florida History Prevails in Everglades City." *South Florida Sun Sentinel*, August 17, 2003.

———. "Trails Will Help Titusville Recruit Aerospace." *Florida Today*, May 24, 2016.

Hollis, Tim. *Florida's Miracle Strip.* Jackson: University Press of Mississippi, 2004.

Honeymoon Island State Park. "History of Honeymoon Island." Florida State Parks, accessed September 4, 2020. https://www.floridastateparks.org/parks-and-trails/honeymoon-island-state-park/history.

Indian River Lagoon National Estuary Program. "One Lagoon. One Future." One Lagoon, accessed February 17, 2022. https://onelagoon.org/.

Jaccard, Deon Lawrance. *The Historic Splendor of Amelia Island*. Fernandina, FL: Amelia Island Museum of History, 1997.

"Jax Facts." Visit Jacksonville and the Beaches, accessed December 1, 2021. https://www.visitjacksonville.com/about/jax-facts/.

J.N. "Ding" Darling National Wildlife Refuge. "About the Refuge." US Fish and Wildlife Service, accessed October 15, 2020. https://www.fws.gov/refuge/JN_Ding_Darling/about.html.

Kane, Harnett T. *The Golden Coast*. Garden City, NY: Doubleday, 1959.

Kaye, Ken, and *Sun Sentinel*. "Solving Mystery of 'Lost City' in Everglades." *South Florida Sun Sentinel*, May 18, 2014.

Klein, H. C. "Who Came up with 'The World's Luckiest Fishing Village'?" *Destin Log*, October 25, 2016.

Kolianos, Phyllis E. and Brent R. Weisman (editors). *The Lost Florida Manuscript of Frank Hamilton Cushing*. Gainesville: University Press of Florida, 2005.

Lanier, Sidney. *Florida: Its Scenery, Climate, and History*. Philadelphia: Lippincott, 1876.

Lindbergh, Anne Morrow. *Gift from the Sea*. New York: Pantheon, 1955.

Mesa, Bianca. "Lancelot Jones, Soul of an Ecological Jewel." *Miami Times*, September 30, 2020.

Messier, Hannah. "Hope the Sea Turtle Recovering at Gulf Specimen Marine Lab after Being Beached by Red Tide." Tallahassee: WCTV, October 27, 2021.

"Miami at 100." *Miami Herald* Special Section, July 21, 1996.

Miller, Mike. "Satellite Beach, Florida." Florida Back Roads Travel, December 16, 2021. Accessed March 2, 2022. https://www.florida-backroads-travel.com/satellite-beach-florida.html.

———. "Seaside, Florida: The Definition of New Urbanism." Florida Back Roads Travel, updated June 7, 2022, accessed July 30, 2020. https://www.florida-backroads-travel.com/seaside-florida.html.

Morris, Allen. *Florida Place Names*. Coral Gables: University of Miami Press, 1974.

National Oceanic and Atmospheric Administration. "Coral Reef Condition: A Status Report for Florida's Coral Reef." 2020 release of 2014–2018 data. https://www.coris.noaa.gov/monitoring/status_report/docs/FL_508_compliant.pdf.

National Park Service. "The History of Castillo de San Marcos: From Contemporary Narratives and Letters." Source Book Series Number 3, Reprint 1955. https://www.nps.gov/parkhistory/online_books/source/sb3/sb3toc.htm.

———. "*Urca de Lima* Shipwreck." Accessed December 29, 2021. https://www.nps.gov/articles/urcadelima.htm.

NWF Daily News. "Editorial: Who Owns the 'Emerald Coast'?" June 29, 2011.

Packard, Winthrop. *Florida Trails*. Boston: Small, Maynard, 1910.

Paisley, Clifton. *The Red Hills of Florida, 1528–1865*. Tuscaloosa: University of Alabama Press, 1989.

Palace Saloon. "About the Palace Saloon." Accessed January 25, 2022. http://thepalacesaloon.com/.

Pfankuch, T. Bart. "How Little Lanark Village Helped Save the World." *Tallahassee Magazine*, November 5, 2015.

Pierce, Charles W. *Pioneer Life in Southeast Florida*. Coral Gables: University of Miami Press, 1970.

Pittman, Craig. "How the CIA Took over a Florida Island." CrimeReads, December 1, 2021. Accessed December 27, 2021. https://crimereads.com/how-the-cia-took-over-a-florida-island/.

———. *Oh, Florida!* New York: St. Martin's Press, 2017.

Read, William A. *Florida Place Names of Indian Origin and Seminole Personal Names*. Tuscaloosa: University of Alabama Press, 2004.

Remington, Frederic. "Cracker Cowboys of Florida." *Harpers*, August 1895.

Rountree, Bob. "The Savannas: An Unlikely Oasis." Florida Rambler, accessed December 21, 2021. https://www.floridarambler.com/florida-camping/savannas-recreation-area/.

Rudloe, Jack. *The Living Dock*. Golden, CO: Fulcrum Press, 1988.

Seminole Tribe of Florida. "Egmont Key: A Seminole Story." Clewiston, FL: Tribal Historic Preservation Office, 2017.

Spencer, Hullin. "Spinners of Gold in Florida." *Suniland Magazine*, November 1925.

St. Andrews State Park. "St. Andrews State Park History." Accessed July 29, 2020. https://www.floridastateparks.org/parks-and-trails/st-andrews-state-park/history.

St. Augustine Alligator Farm and Zoological Park. "Our History." Accessed December 31, 2021. https://www.alligatorfarm.com/our-history/.

St. Johns County Tourist Development Council. "St. Johns County TDC Visitor Tracking Report: January–March 2020." Accessed June 24, 2022. https://s3.us-east-1.amazonaws.com/st-augustine-2019/images/SAPVB-doc-images/St.-Johns-County-January-March-2020-Visitor-Tracking-Report-FINAL.pdf?v=1620061130.

Beach stumps of coastal pine trees are indicative of rising sea levels along Florida's coast.

St. Vincent National Wildlife Refuge. "St. Vincent National Wildlife Refuge." US Fish and Wildlife Service, accessed August 23, 2020. https://www.fws.gov/refuge/st_vincent/.

Staletovich, Jenny. "Lloyd Miller Who Helped Found Biscayne National Park, Dies at 100." WRLN 91.3 FM, August 26, 2020. https://www.wlrn.org/2020-08-26/lloyd-miller-who-helped-found-biscayne-national-park-dies-at-100.

Stockbridge, Frank Parker, and John Holliday Perry. *So This Is Florida*. Jacksonville, FL: Perry, 1938.

Taylor, Thomas W. *Florida's Territorial Lighthouses, 1821–1845: A Legacy of Concern for the Mariner*. Daytona Beach, FL: Burgman, ca. 1995.

Tebeau, Charlton W. *Florida's Last Frontier: The History of Collier County*. Coral Gables: University of Miami Press, 1957.

———. *Man in the Everglades: 2,000 Years of Human History in the Everglades National Park*. Rev. 2nd ed. Coral Gables: University of Miami Press, 1968.

Timucuan Ecological and Historic Preserve. "Anna's Manumission and Will." National Park Service, accessed December 21, 2021. https://www.nps.gov/timu/learn/historyculture/kp_anna_manumission_will.htm.

———. "Visiting Kingsley Plantation." National Park Service, accessed December 2, 2021. https://www.nps.gov/timu/learn/historyculture/kp_visiting.htm.

Tinsley, Jim Bob. *Florida Cow Hunter: The Life and Times of Bone Mizell*. Gainesville: University Press of Florida, 1990.

Townsend, Richard F., and Robert V. Sharp, eds. *Hero, Hawk, and Open Hand: American Indian Art of the Ancient Midwest and South*. New Haven, CT, and London: Yale University Press, in association with the Art Institute of Chicago, ca. 2004.

US Fish and Wildlife Service. "Pelican Island National Wildlife Refuge." Accessed August 23, 2020. https://www.fws.gov/refuge/pelican_island/.

Walk, Deborah. "Sarasota's Circus Legacy Lives On!" The Ringling, accessed August 30, 2020. https://www.ringling.org/sarasotas-circus-legacy-lives.

Wapling, Greg. "Land Speed Racing History: Daytona Beach Road Course." Hot Rods Down Under, accessed November 23, 2021. https://www.gregwapling.com/hotrod/land-speed-racing-history/land-speed-racing-daytona-beach.html.

Waterbury, Jean Parker, ed. *The Oldest City: St. Augustine*. St. Augustine, FL: St. Augustine Historical Society, 1983.

WaterColor. "Welcome to WaterColor: A Southern Coastal Landscape." Accessed August 1, 2020. https://www.joe.com/community/watercolor.

Watts, Betty M. *The Watery Wilderness of Apalach, Florida*. Tallahassee, FL: Apalach Books, 1975.

Whitney, Ellie, D. Bruce Means, and Anne Rudloe. *Priceless Florida: Natural Ecosystems and Native Species*. Sarasota, FL: Pineapple Press, 2004.

Williams, Lindsey, and U. S. Cleveland. *Our Fascinating Past: Charlotte Harbor—the Early Years*. Punta Gorda, FL: Charlotte Harbor Area Historical Society, 1993.

Winter, Nevin O. *Florida: The Land of Enchantment*. Boston: Page, 1918.

Work Projects Administration. *Florida: A Guide to the Southernmost State*. New York: Oxford University Press, 1939.

Wynne, Lewis N. "Pigs Will Wallow in the Streets: The Rise and Demise of Cedar Key as Florida's Port City." *Gulf Coast Historical Review* (Fall 1994): 44–59.

Young, Robin. "Mexico Beach, Florida, Motel Owner Describes Michael's Fierce Winds and Floodwaters." Here and Now, October 15, 2018. https://www.wbur.org/hereandnow/2018/10/15/hurricane-michael-mexico-beach-florida

INDEX

A. L. Lewis Museum, 135
Accord Civil Rights Museum, 128
Adams Key Environmental Education Center, 94
Ais Indians, 104-5
Akin, Edward, 87
Alcazar Hotel, St. Augustine, 129
Allan, Henry C., 21
Alligator Harbor, *28*
alligator, *68*
Amelia Island State Park, 142
Amelia Island, 7, 134-42
Amelia River, 134
American Beach, 135
Anastasia Island State Park, 131
Anastasia Island, 124, 131
Apache Indians, 127
Apalachee Bay, 34, 37
Apalachee Indians, 24, 34
Apalachicola Bay, 16-21, 27, 29, *146*
Apalachicola River, 10, 27, 29, 128
Apalachicola Sponge Exchange, 29
Apalachicola, 14, *26*, 29
Apollo 11, 114
Apollo Beach, 117
Arcadia, 70
Aripeka, 32
Atlantic Ocean, 7, 127, 139
Atlantic to Gulf Railroad, 141
Aucilla River, 32
Audubon of Florida, 121-22
Audubon, John James, 79

Bahamas, 76
Bahamians, 87
Bahia Honda Bridge, 83
Bailey-Matthews National Shell Museum, 61
bald eagle, 36, 45, 77, *121*
Bald Point State Park, 27
Barber, Joe, 18-19
Barbour, George M., 37

Barefoot Mailmen, 109
Barnell, Dennis, 16
Barron River, 75, *75*
Bernier, Katie, 72
Betsch, MaVynee, 135
Bickel, Karl A., 60, 67
Big Bend Saltwater Paddling Trail, 32
Big Cypress National Preserve, 69
Big Pine Key, 81
Big Talbot Island State Park, 7, 142, 145, *143, 144, 145*
Bill Baggs Cape Florida State Park, *98, 99, 100*, 101
Biscayne Bay, 7, *90, 93, 94, 95, 101*, 91-101, 108
Biscayne National Park Institute, 94
Biscayne National Park, 91-101
Black Caesar, 87
Blackrock Beach, 142, *144*
Blowing Rocks Preserve, 7, 111, *111*
Boca Chita Key, 7, *90, 95*
Boca Chita Lighthouse, *90, 95*
Boca Grande Pass, 60
Bonaparte, Napoleon, 72
Bonita Beach, 37
Bonneville Salt Flats, Utah, 116
Bowles, William Augustus, 34
Bradenton, 43, 46
Bremen, Gary, *92*, 92-94
Brevard County, 109, 112, 117
Bridgeport, Connecticut, 46
Buffet, Jimmy, 60
Bujalski, Julie Ward, 52
Bulow Plantation Ruins Historic State Park, 132

Ca' d'Zan Venetian gothic mansion, Sarasota, 46, *47*
Cabbage Key Inn Restaurant, 60
Cabbage Key, 60
Caladesi Island State Park, 45

Calusa Indians, *56,* 57-59, *59,* 65, 66, 87; shell middens of, 64, *64*
Camp Gordon Johnston, 21
Camp Helen State Park, 10, *10*
Canaveral National Seashore, 116-117, *117*
Cape Canaveral, 104, 112, 140
Cape Florida Lighthouse, 87, *98*
Cape Sable Augerdent, 76
Cape Sable seaside sparrow, 75
Cape Sable, 69, 75-76
Cape San Blas, 7, 14, 19, 21, *23*, 117
Cape St. George Lighthouse, 16-18, *18, 19,* 20
Cape St. George, 16-19
Capece, John C., 146
Capone, Al, 35, 72
Captiva Island, 60, 62-65
Carey, Jim, 12
Caribbean, 31, 45, 81, 88, 89
Carlisle Indian School, Pennsylvania, 127
Carlos, King (Calusa chief), 58
Carman, Karl, 92
Carr, Archie, 88, 120
Carrabelle, 18-21
Castillo de San Marcos, St. Augustine, 124-27, *128,* 131
Cayo Costa State Park, 60
Cedar Key, 32, 34, 37-38, *39,* 141
Central America, 89
Central Intelligence Agency (CIA), 65
Century Magazine, 120
Cerulean, Susan, 27
Chapman, Frank, 120, 123
Charles, Ray, 132
Charleston Earthquake, 37
Charlotte Harbor, 60
Chassahowitzka National Wildlife Refuge, 41

Chassahowitzka Wildlife
Management Area, 41
Chatham Bend Key, Everglades
National Park, 70, 76
Chattahoochee River, 10, 29
Chekika (Seminole war leader),
87
Chicago, 5, 35, 135
Choctawhatchee Bay, 14
Chokoloskee, 66, 70-71
Civil War, 16, 29, 37, 47, 62,
135; Everglades region and,
72; Fort Clinch and, 141;
St. Augustine and, 127
Civilian Conservation Corps,
141
Clearwater, 43, 45, 50
Cocoa Village, 119
Collier County, 74
Collier, Barron Gift, 74
Collins, Leroy, 15
Colonial Quarter, St.
Augustine, *124*, 128-29
coral reefs, 81, 148
Cortez (town), 50-52, *50*
Creature from the Black Lagoon,
133
Crooked River Lighthouse,
20, 20
Crystal River, 32, 40-41, 120
Cuba, 48, 128; Flamingo
history and, 76; Paradise
Coast history and, 58-59
Cultural Coast, 43, 45-46,
48-50
Cumberland Island, 135, 140
Cumberland Sound, 141
Cushing, Frank Hamilton, 57

Dade County, 92-93
Darling, Jay Norwood "Ding,"
56, 62, 64
Davis, Jack, 89
Davis, Jefferson, 141
Daytona Beach, 116, *116*
De Aviles, Don Pedro
Menendez, 124, 137
De Leon, Juan Ponce, 58
De Lima, Miguel, 102
De Narvaez, Panfilo, 34
De Salmon, Don Francisco,
104
De Soto National Memorial,
46
De Soto, Hernando, 34, 46
De Vaca, Cabeza, 34
Deepwater Horizon Spill, 148

Delaney, John, 136
Destin, 7, 14-15
Dickinson, Jonathan, 105
Dier, Andrew, 11
Disney World, 38
Dixie Highway, 97, 119
Doc Ford's Restaurant,
Sanibel, 65
Dog Island, 27
dolphins, 7, 12, 13, 57, 72,
147; Biscayne Bay and, *94,*
95; Marineland and, 133,
133; statue of, *53*
Douglas, Marjory Stoneman,
69
Drake, Sir Francis, 124
Dry Tortugas, 81
DuBois Park, 105
Duck Stamp Program, 62
Dunedin, 52, *53*, 55, 115
Duval County, 136

East Coast Greenway, 114, 142
East Coast Railroad, 86, 95,
109
Eau Gallie Arts District, 119
Eden Gardens State Park, *14*
Edison, Thomas, 62
Egmont Key Ferry, 48
Egmont Key, 46-48
Eller, Jodi, 14
Elliott Key, 7, 91, 92
Emerald Coast, 9-15, *11*
Empire Mica, 19
England, 46, 88, 124, 135
Estero Bay, 58, *59*
Everglades, 7, 31, 66-77, *67,*
96
Everglades City, 67, 69, 72-75,
73, 75, 76
Everglades National Park, 7,
66-77, *67, 96*
Everglades: River of Grass
(Douglas), 69

Fascell, Dante, 92
Faver-Dykes State Park, 132
Federal Writers Project, 8, 10,
125
Ferdinand VII (Spanish king),
135
Fernandina Beach, 135, 139-
141
Finest Kind (Green), 51
Fire, Felix, 131
First Coast, 124, 128, 133-35
Fisher, Carl, 96-97

Fisher, Jane, 96-97
Flagler Beach, 132
Flagler College, 129
Flagler Station Over-Sea
Railway Historeum, 83
Flagler, Henry, 7, 82-87, 95-
96, 109, 124, 129-30
Flamingo, 69, 75-77
Florida A1A, 133, 134
Florida Audubon Society. *See*
Audubon of Florida
Florida Bay, 7, 69-72, 76-77
Florida Circumnavigational
Saltwater Paddling Trail, 5,
13-14, 69, 72; map of, *5*
Florida Coast-to-Coast Trail,
114
Florida cowboys, 48-50
*Florida for Tourists, Invalids, and
Settlers* (Barbour), 37
Florida Greenways and Trails
Council, 115
Florida Keys National Marine
Sanctuary, 81
Florida Keys Overseas Heritage
Trail, 86
Florida Keys, 7, 74, 76, 78-89,
141; biological diversity of,
81-82; Overseas Railroad
of, 83-87; turtling in, 88-89;
wrecking along, 87-88
Florida Museum of Natural
History, *57*
Florida National Scenic Trail,
69
Florida Office of Greenways
and Trails, 72
Florida Panhandle, 5, 24
Florida panther, 69
Florida School of the Deaf and
Blind, St. Augustine, 129
Florida State University Marine
Laboratory, 19
Florida Today, 113
Florida: A Guide to the
Southernmost State (Work
Projects Administration),
8, 125
*Florida's Last Frontier: The
History of Collier County*
(Tebeau), 74
Florida's Miracle Strip (Hollis),
11
Forbes Grant, 24
Ford, Henry, 62
Forgotten Coast, *2*, 5, 7, 16-
29, *17, 25, 28*

Fort Caroline National Memorial, 136-37, *137*
Fort Clinch State Park, 5, 14, *141*, 141-42
Fort Dade, 47
Fort De Soto Park, *6*, 42
Fort George Island, 137
Fort George River, 139
Fort Marion. *See* Castillo de San Marcos
Fort Matanzas National Monument, 124, *126*, 127
Fort Mose Historic State Park, 127-28, *129*
Fort Pierce, 102, 104, 110, 112
Fort Walton Beach, *11*, 12
Four Months in a Sneak-Box (Bishop), 17
Fox, Charles Donald, 97, 109
France, 74, 124, 136-37

Gamble Rogers Memorial State Recreation Area, 132
Garden Street, Titusville, 114
Gaspar, Jose (Gasparilla), 62, 72
George II (English king), 135
Georgia, 5, 14, 29, 34, 128, 131
Germany, 46
Ghost Village, Everglades, 72
Gift from the Sea (Lindbergh), 62
Gilbert's Bar House of Refuge, *106, 107,* 107
Glenn, John, 112
The Golden Coast (Kane), 50-51, 79
Gomez, Juan, 72
Goofy Golf, 12
gopher tortoise, 48, *48,* 75
Goss, Porter, 65
Governor's House Cultural Center and Museum, 128
Granday, Armand, 89
Grayton Beach State Park, 12
Great blue heron, *6*
Great Depression, 101
Great Wine Wreck, 108
green sea turtle, 88, 109
Green, Ben, 51
Greenberg, Margaret, 64
Greene, Juanita, 92
Guana Tolomato Matanzas National Estuarine Research Reserve, 131
The Gulf (Davis), 89

Gulf Coast fritillary butterfly, *39*
Gulf of Mexico, 29, 69
Gulf Specimen Marine Lab, 148-49
Gulf Stream, 103, 108, 109, 137
Gulf sturgeon, 32
Gulf View Motel, Mexico Beach, 22
Gulf World Marine Park, 12
Gulfarium, 12

Hamilton, James "Ed," 109
Harding, Warren, 93, 97
Harpers, 49
Hatch, George, 24
Haulover Beach, 117
Haulover Canal, *115*
Havana, 103-5, 139
hawksbill sea turtle, 108, 109
Hernandez, Jose, 132
Hiller, Herb, 67, 113
Hillman, Eleanor, 18
Hillsboro Inlet, 109
Historic Coast, 124, 135
The Historic Splendor of Amelia Island (Jaccard), 134
Ho-Hum RV Park, *2*
Hollis, Tim, 11
Homestead Air Reserve Station, 93
Homosassa Springs, 40-41
Honest Johns Fish Camp, 119
Honeymoon Island State Park, *42, 51,* 52
Honeymoon Island, *42, 51,* 52
Hooppell, Nick, 24
Hoover, Herbert Jr., 91-92
Hoover, Herbert, 93
Hope (loggerhead sea turtle), 148-49, *149*
Horseshoe Beach, 32
horseshoe crab, 32, 145
House Intelligence Committee, 65
Huff, Patty, 72-74, *73*
Huff, Steve, *73,* 74
Huguenots, 136
Hurricane Andrew, 22, 94
Hurricane Donna, 74
Hurricane Michael, 22-24
Hutchison Island, 107
Hypoluxo, 108

Indian Key, 58, 87

Indian River Area Preservation League, 122
Indian River Lagoon, *115*, 115-16, 119-23
Ingraham, F. E., 96
Intracoastal Waterway, 14, 131, 136
Isabella (Spanish queen), 58
Isle of Eight Flags Shrimp Festival, Fernandina Beach, 140
Italy, 46, 74

J.N. "Ding" Darling National Wildlife Refuge, *63, 64,* 64, 120
Jaccard, Deon Lawrence, 134
Jackson, Andrew, 35, 135
Jacksonville, 135-36, 139
Jensen Beach, 110
John and Mable Ringling Museum of Art. *See* The Ringling
Johns, Willie, 47-48
Johnson, Walt, 115
Jones, Sir Lancelot, 93-94
Jug Island, 32
Jungle Trail, 123
Jupiter, 7, 105, 113-14
Jupiter Inlet, 7, 105
Jupiter Inlet Lighthouse & Museum, 105, *111*

Kane, Harnett, T., 50, 79
Keaton Beach, 32
Keene, Matt, *13,* 14
Kemp's ridley sea turtle, 31, 109
key deer, 81-82
Key Largo, 86, 91
Key Marco, 57-58
Key West Gazette, 86
Key West Terminal, 86
Key West, 5, 46, 78, *80, 81,* 80-81, 86-89, *89,* 142
Kingsley Plantation, *138,* 139
Kingsley, Zephaniah, 139
Kissimmee Waterkeeper, 146
Knight's Key, 83
Knights Key-Moser Channel Bridge, 83
Kroegel, Paul, 120-121

Labor Day Hurricane of 1935, 86
Lake Okeechobee, 47
Lake Worth, 108

Lanark Village, 21
Lanier, Sidney, 130
Largo, 43, 86
leatherback sea turtle, 108-9
Lewis, A. L., 135
Lightsey Museum, St. Augustine, 129
Lindbergh, Anne Morrow, 62
Lindbergh, Charles, 62
Little Talbot Island State Park, 136, 142, *142, 145*
The Living Dock (Rudloe), 32
loggerhead sea turtle, 108-9, *110, 148-49, 149*
Long Key Viaduct, Florida Keys, 83
Looe Key coral reef, Florida Keys, *82*
Lost City, Everglades, 72. *See also* Ghost Village

Madison Square Garden, 46
Maine, 114, 142
Malabar, 123
Mallory Square, Key West, 78, *80*
manatee, 7, 32, 57, 72, 81, 116; in Crystal River, *40,* 40-41
Mangiapia, Mary, 13
mangrove, 7, 42-45, *43,* 58; historic description of in Everglades, 67; islands of in Indian River Lagoon, 115, *115*; mangrove tunnels in Keys, 81, 89; Pelican Island and, 119, *119*; removal of on Miami Beach, 96
The Mangrove Coast (Bickel), 60, 67
Marathon, 83
Marco Island, 7, 57
Margaret Street, Key West, 89
Marianna, 22, 24
Marineland, 133, *133*
Marks, Charles, 24
marsh hawk, *45*
Marsh, Fred Dana, 133
Martin County, 107
Matanzas Inlet, 127
Matanzas River, 131
Matthiessen, Peter, 70
McLarty Treasure Museum, Sebastian Inlet State Park, 105
Melbourne Beach, 109, 119

Merritt Island National Wildlife Refuge, 114-15, *115*
Mexico Beach, 14, 21-22
Mexico, 34, 45, 103; Mexico City, 34
Mexico City, 34
Miami Beach, 96-97, 101
Miami blue butterfly, 82
Miami Herald, 65, 92
Miami, 7, 74, 86, 90, 117; Barefoot Mailmen and, 108-9; Biscayne Bay and, 91-101
Millay, Edna St. Vincent, 62
Miller, Lloyd, 93
Miracle Strip Amusement Park, Panama City Beach, 12
Mississippi River, 10
Morabal, Jean (Blue), 78, *80*
Morro Castle, Cuba, 103
Mosquito Lagoon, 5, 116, 118, *122*
Mound Key, 58, *59*
Mount Trashmore, 93
Muir, John, 93
Muscogee Creek Indians, 33, 34, 41, 110
Museum of Florida History, *103*
My Nature Nook (Blatchley), 42
Myakka River, 60

Nana (Florida's highest sand dune), 135
NASCAR, 116
Nassau County, 135
National Park Service, 118, 139, 144
National Park System, 91
National Register of Historic Places, 139
National Wildlife Refuge System, 120, 123
Nature Coast, 7, 27, 30-41, *30, 33, 36*
Nature Conservancy, 27, 111
Nature on Sanibel (Greenberg), 64
Nature's Giant Fish Bowl, Homosassa Springs State Park, 41
Negro Travelers' Green Book, 136
New England fishermen, 59
New Urbanism, 12
No Name Key, Florida Keys, 81
Nocoroco village site, Tomoka State Park, 133

North Atlantic right whale, 140-41
North Carolina coast, 24
Nostalgic Florida (Alderson), 97

Oak Hill Mound, 118
Oak Hill, 118
Oasis Visitor Center, Biscayne National Park, 69
Ocean Aid 360, 147
Ochlockonee Bay, 27
Ochlockonee River, 27
Ochopee, 72
Oh, Florida! (Pittman), 146
Ohio Key, Florida Keys, 83
Okaloosa County, 11
Oklahoma, 47, 70
Oleta River State Park, 101
Orioles (early Spanish governor in St. Augustine), 105
Ormond Beach, 116
Osprey Trail, *51,* 52
osprey, 31, *35,* 52, 69, 77, *134, 147*
Overseas Highway, Florida Keys, 86, 89
Overseas Railroad, 82, *84*

Palace Saloon, Fernandina Beach, *140,* 140
Paleo Indians, 33, 57
Palm Beach, 108
Panacea, *16,* 32, 148
Panama Canal, 86
Panama City Beach, 10, 12
Panama City, *8,* 9-11, 22
Panther Key, 72
Paradise Coast, 58
Parker, Polly, 47-48
Pass-a-Grille, *49,* 50, *55*
Peace River, 60
Pelican Island National Wildlife Refuge, 119-123, *119*
Pelican Island Wildlife Festival, 120
pelican, brown, 45, *50,* 52, *119,* 119-20
pelican, white, 36, *63,* 64, 69, 120
Pellicer Creek, 132
Pensacola, 7, 8, 10-12, 14
Penton, Dan, 33
Perry, John Holliday, 3, 81, 90
Peru, 103
Petticoat Junction, Panama City Beach, 12

Pierce, Charles W., 108
Pierce, Dr. Ray, 24, 27
Pigeon Key, Florida Keys, *83*, 83
Pine Island, 58, 120
Pinellas County, 7, 31, 43, 45, 52
Pinellas Trail, 52, 55
Piney Island, Forgotten Coast, *17*
Pioneer Life in Southeast Florida (Pierce), 108
Pirate & Treasure Museum, St. Augustine, 128, 130
Pittman, Craig, 146
Plant, Henry, 86
Plate Fleet, *102*, 103
Playalinda Beach, Canaveral National Seashore, 117
Pompano Beach, 108
Ponce de Leon Hotel, St. Augustine, 129-30
Porgy Key, Biscayne Bay, 93-94
Port St. Lucie, 110
Porter, Edward G., 18
Preservation Project Jacksonville, 136
Princess Place Preserve, 132
Prohibition, 35, 140
Providencia, Spanish ship, 108
Punta Gorda, 48-49
Punta Rassa, 48

Railroad Museum, Florida Keys, 83
Randell Research Center, Pine Island, 58
Rash, Steve, 29
Rawlings, Marjorie Kinnan, 136
red tide, 60, 148-49
red wolf, 27
Reddington, George, 131
Remington, Frederic, 49
Revenge of the Creature, 133
Ribault, Jean, 137
Ringling, The, 46
Ringling Brothers and Barnum & Bailey Circus, 46
Ringling, John, 46
River of Grass. *See* Everglades National Park
Road to Nowhere, *36*, 36
Rockefeller, John D., 86
Roosevelt, Theodore, 62, 119, 120

Rountree, Bob, 110
Route A1A, 134
Rudloe, Cypress, 148
Rudloe, Jack, 32, 149
Ruskin, 43

salvagers, 87
Sam's Mound, 118
San Francisco Earthquake, 135
San Pedro Underwater Archeological Preserve State Park, 87
Sanibel Island, 58, 60-65, *61*, *62, 63, 65*
Sarasota Bay, 46, 50
Sarasota, 43, 45-46, *47*, 49
Satellite Beach, 112
Savannahs Preserve State Park, 110
sawfish, 69
Schaus' swallowtail butterfly, 82
sea beans, 61
Sea World, 133
Seadade, 91
Seahorse Key, *38*
Seaside, 12
Sebastian Fishing Museum, 109
Sebastian Inlet State Park, 105
Sebastian Inlet, 103, 105
Sebastian, 119, 120
Second Seminole War, 58, 72, 87, 127, 132
Seminole Indians, 24, 33, 35, 41, 58, 62, 100, 118, 133; Chekika (Seminole war leader), 87; Egmont Key imprisonment, 47-48; in Everglades, 66, 69-70; Parker, Polly, 47-48; salvaging shipwrecks, 87, 108; Second Seminole War, 58, 72, 87, 127, 132; Third Seminole War, 47-48; Wildcat (Seminole war leader), 127
Seminole Rest, Canaveral National Seashore, *118*, 118
Seminole Tribune, 47
Seven Mile Bridge, Florida Keys, 82-83, *84*, 86
Seville, Spain, 103
Shark Valley, Everglades National Park, *67, 68*, 69
Shell Mound, Cedar Key, 34
shipwrecks, 61, 87, 88, 103-108

Simpson's Creek, 142, 145
Sink Creek, Nature Coast, *36*
Sisters, The. *See* Casa Ybel, Sanibel Island
Skid Row, New York, 87
Skunk Ape Headquarters, Ochopee, 72
Sloppy Joe's Bar, Key West, *89*
Smallwood, Ted, 66
Smallwoods Store Museum, 66, *68*, 71
Smith, Charles, 22-24
Smithsonian, 57
Snake-a-Torium, Panama City Beach, 12
So Excellent a Fishe (Carr), 88
So This Is Florida (Parker and Perry), 3, 81, 90
South America, 45, 105
South Florida Sun Sentinel, 67
South Melbourne Beach, 119
Space Coast, 114
space shuttle, 114
Spain, 35, 87; Calusa relationship with, 58; Ferdinand VII (Spanish king), 135; fighting the French, 137; laws regarding free people of color, 139; Narvaez expedition of; 34; Plate Fleet shipwreck from, 103-5; St. Augustine area and, 124-29; The Ringling and, 46
Spanish-American War, 47, 141
Sparks, Liz, 32
Spencer, Hullin, 97
Spite Highway, Biscayne National Park, 92
Spray (Marineland dolphin), 133
Spring Warrior, Nature Coast, 32
St. Andrews Beach, Emerald Coast, *8*
St. Andrews State Park, *8*, 9
St. Augustine Alligator Farm Zoological Park, 131
St. Augustine Lighthouse, 131
St. Augustine, 7, *125*, 135, 139; history of, 124-32, 137; shipwrecks and, 104-5
St. George Island, 16-19, *16*, 27, 148-49, *149*
St. George Island Ferry, 19

St. George Lighthouse
    Association, 16
St. George Street, St.
    Augustine, 124, *125*
St. Joe Company, 12
St. Johns River, 136, 139
St. Johns River-to-Sea Loop,
    114
St. Joseph Peninsula State Park,
    21, 21, 117
St. Marks National Wildlife
    Refuge, 34, 120
St. Marks, 31, 46, 47
St. Marks River, 34
St. Mary's River, 141
St. Petersburg, 43, 50, 52, 114
St. Petersburg Beach, *4*
St. Theresa, 19
St. Vincent Island, 21, 24, 27,
    120
Standard Oil Company, 86
Starr, Belle, 70
Stevens, Snyder, 119
Stevens, Wallace, 60
Stiltsville, Biscayne Bay, *101*
Stockbridge, Frank Parker, 3,
    81, 90
Sugarloaf Keys, Florida Keys,
    81
Sullivan, Billy (Shitty Bill),
    30, 32
Sun Coast, 43, 50
Suniland Magazine, 97
Surf Coast, 116
Suwannee, 32

Tallahassee Democrat, 24
Tallahassee Magazine, 21
Tallahassee, 5, 37
Tamiami Trail, 69, 72, 74
Tampa Bay Pilots Association,
    47
Tampa Bay, *6*, 13, 43, 45-48
Tampa, 38, 43

Tarpon Springs, 50-51, 52
Tebeau, Charlton, 74
Ten Thousand Islands, 5, 7,
    66-75, *71,* 77, 120
Third Seminole War, 47-48
Three Sisters Springs National
    Wildlife Refuge, Crystal
    River, *40*, 41
Timucuan Ecological and
    Historic Preserve, 135, 136,
    138, 139
Timucuan Indians, 118, 133;
    shell middens of, 118
Timucuan Trail, 142
Titusville, 108, 112-15, *113*;
    welcome center of, *114*
Tocabaga Indians, 48
Tollofsen, Theodore, 9
Tombstone Territory, Panama
    City Beach, 12
Tomoka State Park, 133
Topsail Hill Preserve State
    Park, *15*
Treasure Coast, 103-11
The Truman Show, 12
Trust for Public Land, 135
The Truth about Florida (Fox),
    97, 109
Turkey Point Nuclear Power
    Plant, Biscayne Bay, 93
Turtle Mound, Canaveral
    National Seashore, 116
Tuttle, Julia, 95-96, 101
Twain, Mark, 78

Underground Railroad, 34
US 1, 119
US 98, 21
US Coast Guard, 107
US Life-Saving Service. *See* US
    Coast Guard
United States Navy, 87
United States Postal Service,
    108-9

United States Supreme Court,
    29
University of Miami, 92
Upper and Lower Matecumbe
    Keys, Florida Keys, 87

Vilano Beach, *131*, 131
Voices of the Apalachicola (Eidse),
    19
Volusia County, 117

Wakulla River, 34
Wakulla Volcano, 37
Walton County, 11
Washburn, Clinton 52
Washington Oaks Gardens
    State Park, 7, 131-32, *132*
Washington, George, 131
WaterColor, 12
Waters Less Traveled (Alderson),
    32
Watson, Ed, 70-71, 76
Wesley House, Eden Gardens
    State Park, *14*
West Pass, Forgotten Coast,
    16, 24
White, Randy Wayne, 65
Whitfield Estates, 46
Wild Florida Waters (Alderson),
    70
Wildcat (Seminole war leader),
    127
Wilderness Waterway, 69-70
Williams, Tennessee, 78
Wilson, E. O., 146
Winter, Nevin O., 70, 82, 86
World War II, 21, 52, 107,
    141
wreckers, Florida Keys, 87-88

Yankeetown, 32
Young, Louise, 132
Yulee, David Levy, 38, 141

Lone figure on sunset beach.

ABOUT THE AUTHOR

Doug Alderson prefers a kayak to a desk, hugs trees and friends, and loves observing wildlife in their natural environment. Most of his 16 published books focus on the dynamic and quirky nature of his home state of Florida. They include *Florida's Rivers, America's Alligator, Wild Florida Waters, Waters Less Traveled, New Dawn for the Kissimmee River, Encounters with Florida's Endangered Wildlife,* and *A New Guide to Old Florida Attractions,* which the Florida Writers Association placed in the top five of published books for 2017. He has won five first place Royal Palm Literary awards for nonfiction books and several other state and national writing and photography awards.

Doug's articles and photographs have also been published in *Native Peoples, Wildlife Conservation, American Forests, Sea Kayaker, Sierra, Mother Earth News, Shaman's Drum, Campus Life, America, The Old Farmer's Almanac, AT Journeys, Rails to Trails, New Age Travel,* and several others. He has been a featured speaker at symposiums, writer's conferences, and book fairs, and he has appeared in media outlets such as the *New York Times, National Geographic* online, *Boston Globe,* and *Adventure Kayak* magazine for his writing and trail work. He is also an adventurer, having hiked the entire Appalachian Trail, coordinated a group walk across the United States, backpacked through Europe, and mapped a 1,500-mile sea kayaking trail around Florida.